DRAUGHTS OF REMEMBRANCE

DRAUGHTS OF REMEMBRANCE

BY

ANN REE COLTON

ARC PUBLISHING COMPANY
POST OFFICE BOX 1138
GLENDALE, CALIFORNIA 91209

Copyright © 1959 by Ann Ree Colton

All rights reserved, including the right to reproduce this book or portions thereof in any form.

Third Printing

Printed in the United States of America by—
DeVorss & Co., *Publishers*
1641 Lincoln Boulevard, Santa Monica, Calif. 90404

Lovingly Dedicated

To Those Who Made

This Book Possible

ACKNOWLEDGMENT

I wish to express my deep gratitude and thankfulness to Jonathan Murro for his constant encouragement and untiring assistance in creating this written work.

FOREWORD

The many lives a person lives are as jewels strung upon an endless, eternal thread. Each life or jewel is patterned, shaped and cut according to his efforts and experiences on earth. Some jewels are brilliant and dazzling; others are but crude facsimiles of the real. The perfect lives one has lived are waiting to be placed in a central diadem where they may reign in the sovereignty of their accomplishment.

The soul is the record-bearer of former lives. The soul, working with the inner nature of man, strives constantly to blend and coordinate the works of the present life with the unfinished actions of lives formerly lived. The soul is also the bearer of good tidings, for grace earned in former lives will inevitably present itself in ripe or right timing. A person's character is built from the virtues of previous lives. The structure of his character determines what sort of grace and works he may channel to the world.

In the present age the majority of people

are so completely engrossed in their present personalities that it never occurs to them they have lived before. To some persons the reality of re-embodiment or reincarnation is abhorrent, for they find it offensive to think there is a law blueprinting their destinies. Those who cannot hear or bear the thought of repeated lives choose to ignore this truth because it places upon them the responsibility for their own actions, emotions, and thoughts. However, regardless of their beliefs, all persons re-embody; and thus inherit the major compulsions, the basic moods, and the underlying drives from their former lives.

The Lord Jesus understood the reality of re-embodiment or reincarnation. He explained that Elias and John the Baptist were one when He said:

> *"For all the prophets and the law prophesied until John. And if ye will receive it, this is Elias, which was for to come. He that hath ears to hear, let him hear."* —St. Matthew 11:13-15

> *"And Jesus answered and said unto them, Elias truly shall first come, and restore all things. But I say unto you, That Elias is come already, and*

they knew him not, but have done unto him whatsoever they listed. Likewise shall also the Son of man suffer of them. Then the disciples understood that he spake unto them of John the Baptist." —St. Matthew 17:11-13

God has arranged it so that everyone undergoes a renewal of the blood stream every seven years. Also, every seven years a draught of remembrance, relating to past lives, is drawn into certain levels of one's consciousness beneath the surface layer of consciousness. This draught of remembrance adds something which is beyond that gathered from the daily experience in life. The seven-year cycles are called *the etheric cycles* because they are etheric impulses timed by "Our Father which art in heaven." The first portion of this book pertains to the etheric cycles: how the memories of past lives are experienced through the draughts of remembrance working with the etheric cycles; how God's law of absolute justice accompanies the etheric cycles, determining exactly what one needs for his growth, development, and evolvement; and how each etheric cycle contains some initiation, or that is, death to the old and birth to the new. The final portion of the book contains mantramic prayers or mantrams to help one to (1) meet the various crises in life, (2) modify and resolve the chronic, static and stagnant conditions carried over from former or past lives, and (3) recognize and channel the grace earned from good works in past lives.

CONTENTS

FOREWORD i

PART ONE

RECOVERY OF PAST LIVES 1
   Recovery of Past Lives Through Dreams 7
   Intermittent Flashes of Revelation as to Past Lives.. 8
   The Protective Sheaths Surrounding the
      Records of Past Lives 10
   The Ethic of Revelation 11

ETHERIC CYCLES
   Birth to the 7th Year 15
   7th Year to the 14th Year 27
   14th Year to the 21st Year 37
   21st Year to the 28th Year 43
   28th Year to the 35th Year 51
   35th Year to the 42nd Year 60
   42nd Year to the 49th Year 65
   49th Year to the 56th Year 69
   56th Year to the 63rd Year 72
   63rd Year to the 70th Year 75

PART TWO

MANTRAMIC PRAYERS
   Emotional Etheric Grooves 79
   Mental Etheric Clots 80
   The Spoken Mantram 81
   Marriage and the Home 85
   Parents and Children 104
   Feelings and Thoughts 119
   Work and Serving 147
   Healing 159
   Sleep and the Soul 166

SUMMARY
   God's Mighty Justice and Perfect Mercy 176

PART ONE

RECOVERY OF PAST LIVES

All creation stems from the eternal law of birth, death, and rebirth. One who expands his vision into cosmos or space, and views the actions of the galaxies and starry systems of the greater universe, sees that even stars are subjected to beginnings and endings. Man is no exception to this essential and eternal law of birth, death, and rebirth.

The eternal law of God is ever at work to perfect each thing and its kind. The eternal law works through man to individualize him and perfect him, so that he may become a co-creator with God. Each life on earth contains but a thimbleful of knowledge. Aeons, epochs, and ages are necessary for man to incorporate all that the cosmic law has to instruct him; all that families, societies, races, nations, and religions have to teach him; and all that he must learn through personal choice, will, and consciousness. When man has absorbed all that God has prepared for him in this eternity or earth, he shall become a whole person, a righteous man, a son of God.

The eternal law of beginning and ending, of birth, death, and rebirth, is gradated to the cosmic law of cause and effect, night and day, winter and summer, famine and plenty. It is experienced in the emotions of man as love and hate; in his thoughts, as positive and negative; in his will, as right or wrong choice; in the diversity of circumstances, as happiness or unhappiness, pleasure or pain, sorrow or joy, having or not having; in the consequential actions and reactions of good and evil.

The cosmic law of cause and effect relates to the system of the earth and the planets accompanying the earth, to the seasons, the forces of nature, and the four elements—air, earth, fire, and water. The law of retribution pertains to blood and blood ties, ancestry, races, nations, societies, and religions. The law of sowing and reaping relates to the use of personal will and personal choice.

Reincarnation and re-embodiment are sustained and supported by the eternal law of incessant creation, the cosmic law of cause and effect, the law of retribution or "an eye for an eye," and the law of sowing and reaping.

Since the coming of Jesus of Nazareth, certain revelations correlating to the cosmic law of cause and effect have been accelerated; the unresolved debts between blood relationships, races, nations, societies, and religions have been quickened; and the laggard debts of the individual have been intensified. Thus, the agitation in the world has become more acute.

In the present age mankind is offered the opportunity to rectify the transgressions against the cosmic law and the forces of nature. Men and women are being given the opportunity to overcome the trespasses in blood relationships, racial and national associations, societies, and religions. The individual is being given the opportunity to correct the sins or erroneous acts of the personal self.

A sin is that which offends the purity of the

soul. A trespass is an act devoid of reverence and respect for others. A transgression is an offense against the protective laws of nature.

When a person sins or errs against his higher nature, he invokes the law of sowing and reaping; and he reaps with exactitude and justice that in which he has erred. Thus, if a man offends love, he must re-earn love over a period of many lives. If he violates his stewardship in life, he must eat the bitter bread of sorrows. When he trespasses against the ties of blood, the begetting of children, the reverent care of children, the sanctity of the family relationship, his racial placement, or his national responsibilities, he shall be maladjusted and discontented in such associations for many lives.

Until the individual debts of sowing and reaping have been accepted, the trespass debts against family, races, nations, societies, and religions have been recognized, and the transgression debts against the cosmic law are understood, one will return to the world with only a subconscious remembrance of past lives and their meaning as to the plan of God.

Millions of people in the world believe in reincarnation; however, the majority of those who believe in reincarnation are unable to recollect and recover the records of their past lives. To believe in reincarnation is one thing, and to be the recipient of the actual knowledge of former lives is another. When one has proven the logic of reincarnation through every facet of his intellect, and when his heart confirms that he lives many lives, *he will then have the choice either to remain on the plateau of fatalistic and passive belief in reincarnation, or move upward to the actual recovery of previous lives*. The soul works continually to equalize belief with knowledge. When one fails to activate the creative portent accompanying the belief in reincarnation, he remains within fatalistic and passive beliefs. When one responds to the vital discovery aspect within the belief in reincarnation, he rises with the impetus of creative knowledge; and therefore the records of his soul are opened to him.

Many find it impossible to believe in God, life extending beyond death, and in the reality of repeated or successive lives. Such persons live out their lives in a self-imposed anesthesia. Among these are some who, through their own evils, have deliberately drunk a draught of forgetfulness, and thus have sealed themselves away from the eternal vision within their souls. There are others who prefer to depend egotistically upon their personal wills, refusing to accept the disciplinary reminders given by their souls.

If all persons of the earth had remained en rapport with their souls, they would now have an uninterrupted access to the records of their past lives. And there would be a continued awareness pertinent to all lives. Each person would remember previous lives as he remembers yesterday's events or events throughout the present life.

One who recovers the records of his former lives through his own direct experience has access to an unusual mental vitality garnered from the lessons learned in past lives. As a rule, he would find it unnecessary to repeat mistakes of previous lives. Working directly with the soul's equation, he would consciously utilize the actions and experiences of past lives. And he could evaluate the present life situations with an eternal perspective. Remembrance of past lives would enable him to rationalize with a thought process superior to the thought process of just one life. It would enable him to use the logic of former lives so as to research the law of cause and effect, and the eternal law.

Were it not for the indirect absorption of past lives through the etheric cycles and draughts of remembrance, all records of previous lives would be obliterated and lost. Whether a person is aware or unaware of his past lives, his life is colored and stimulated by the draughts of remembrance occurring in regular cyclic intervals throughout each life. Therefore, through the draughts of remembrance, all persons in the world are linked with the rhythmic continuity of eternal life.

RECOVERY OF PAST LIVES THROUGH DREAMS

The memories of past lives are most commonly recovered through the natural, etheric absorption cycles, and through dream experience during sleep. There are seven dream veils in the world of sleep. When a person penetrates one or more of the four higher dream veils, he may be given a clue or key to the memory of a past life. A former life may be determined in a dream drama by such identifying symbols as the style of clothing or wearing apparel, the period of furniture, the architectural design of buildings, or certain scenes and environments in a country or nation.

INTERMITTENT FLASHES OF REVELATION AS TO PAST LIVES

There is a certain type of past life memory which is experienced as a nostalgic longing for an unknown place, such as a country, a city, a building, a scene, a body of water. The memory of a past life may be stirred and activated by the instantaneous recognition of a person met for the first time. This recognition is due to the fact that one has known the person in some former life. Sometimes the recognition is experienced as a deep and trusting love, or it may be experienced as an instantaneous dislike, or an inexplainable, violent hatred. Memory of a past life may also be stirred and activated by the instantaneous recognition of a place seen or visited for the first time. This recognition is due to the fact that one has lived in the same or a similar environment in a previous life. It is possible to recall a past life when one visits or returns to a place or environment where he has lived in a former time. This occurs, however, only when there is some debt to be resolved in the environment, or when some grace is ready to be activated.

Majestic music may produce a recollection of more than one past life when a person is ready to receive direct confirmation as to the truth of repeated or successive lives. A painting or a sculptured form, portraying a particular age or time, may open the record of a previous life, especially if the artist or sculptor lived during the time or age in which the viewer had previously lived. A biographical book or a pointed interest in some historical event may also lift the veil concealing a past life.

THE PROTECTIVE SHEATHS SURROUNDING THE RECORDS OF PAST LIVES

All inactive and dormant records of past lives are insulated by protective sheaths located at the base of the skull. When a person is ripe or ready to recover the records of past lives, the soul will unveil the protective sheaths in an orderly and sequential fashion, which in no manner disturbs or disrupts the rhythmic harmony of expression. When one absorbs the records of past lives through the etheric cycles and draughts of remembrance, certain sheaths are automatically dissolved, and the compulsions from past lives flow into the subconscious levels of the consciousness. The protective sheaths may be compared to thin layers of ice. Sometimes the heat of passion, crisis, or shock melts the protective sheaths sealing away the records of previous lives; and the person is prematurely exposed to the attitudes, thoughts, and emotions of past lives, thus causing him or her to undergo a startling transition in personality.

The protective sheaths surrounding the

records of past lives are disturbed and disorganized by inordinate psychic pressure produced through the practice of mediumship. Also, these sheaths are violated by exploitation and experimentation through hypnosis. To seek to recover the records of past lives through any form of hypnosis, drugs, or mediumship affords knowledge only of an inferior and subtle nature, and deranges the co-ordinated, sequential memory of former lives. Such precocious practices prevent the person from receiving the particular lesson accompanying the record of each life. When one persists in hypnotic suggestions or mediumistic probings to penetrate the records of past lives, the result will be inaccuracy, mental confusion, hysteria and, in some instances, obsession. To tamper with the delicate protective sheaths surrounding the records of past lives is to interfere with the rhythmic order and continuity of the soul's action.

THE ETHIC OF REVELATION

Through the draughts of remembrance, the records of former lives seep upward from the darkened depths of the subconscious into the actions, emotions, and thoughts at regular cyclic intervals. When one dreams of past lives, the soul unveils the subconscious, and the records of past lives enter the conscience. When one has intermittent flashes of revelation as to past lives, the soul moves the records of past lives more closely to the waking consciousness. When one opens the records of his five previous lives, he has achieved an illuminative communicableness with the soul. Henceforth, he must tread carefully, gently, for he shall also begin to look into the souls of others and discern the records of their past lives.

The power to reveal past lives is a sacred responsibility. Those who are competent to open the records of past lives have earned this competency through spiritual aptitudes over many lives. Through the illumination faculty of their souls, they may perceive the records of their own past lives and the past lives of others. Such persons must pray continually for guidance, so that they will not offend the ethic of revelation; for to reveal a past life to another before the soul of the person has prepared him to accept the lesson of the life disclosed will endanger the moral, emotional, and mental equilibrium of the person. To disclose a past life to another in wrong timing will release an avalanche of circumstances which may require many lives to remedy. One who repeatedly reveals past lives to others out of timing will paralyze and annul the power to open the records of past lives.

Those who observe the ethic of revelation refrain from revealing the identity of a previous personality to anyone who has a tendency toward egotism, intellectual curiosity, or emotional immaturity; for to reveal the exact identity of a past or previous life to an excitable mind will induce a magnification of the imaginative process, and thus defeat the therapeutic help accompanying the knowledge of a past life.

An indiscriminate person who, through careless conversation, broadcasts his previous lives to others, offends the ethic of revelation and pulls down a curtain between him and further revelation.

If one has observed the ethic of revelation in past lives but is unable in this life to recover the records of his former lives, his soul will lead him to a dedicated person who is qualified to perceive the records of his past lives. The dedicated person will clarify his dream symbols and intermittent flashes as to past lives; and he will help him to correlate the lessons and grace of his five just previous lives with the lessons of the present life.

FIRST ETHERIC CYCLE

Birth to the 7th Year

Some children enter the world with strong, indomitable wills; some children are sensitive, uncertain; while others bring a wholesome, effervescent joy. In these traits may be perceived the reflection of previous lives. Each child has lived in many previous existences or lives on earth; the present life is but a new chapter to be written out of the material at hand.

The unalterable law of balance, working through procreation and conception, directs a child to the environment needed for his soul's expression. Thus there is no accidental placement at birth. A child is placed in an ancestral pattern because this pattern reflects in some degree that which he has been in previous lives. While he may inherit the tendencies of his ancestors, there is, however, a more significant inheritance than that of blood inheritance. It is the inheritance received directly from the soul's record, which reflects former or previous lives.

A child's grace from former lives may place him in an environment with loving parents. If a child has earned the grace to attract parents who have reverent love for one another, he faces the first etheric cycle with a fortified balance. His soul is strengthened by the healthy association of being wanted, directed, loved. If a child's inheritance from his previous lives is basic goodness, he will find himself with honest parents who will sacrifice for him and endeavor in every way to rear him to blend with the higher standards of the world. If in former lives one has been irreverent or neglectful toward life-bearing or life-giving, or has offended the sexual laws, he will be more likely to attract irreverent and inconsiderate parents.

A person who in previous lives has reached a high degree of reverence and evolvement may sometimes choose to be born to agnostic parents, so that his wholesome and reverent actions and attitudes may in time become contagious to them. It is usually the case that he has been with them in some loving association in a former life.

If in the just previous life a person has had atheistic inclinations and a wavering faith, he may be born to agnostic parents with hardened hearts. Upon his reaching maturity, he will have difficulty in organizing his understanding and assembling his loyalties; and he will undergo extended periods of analytical probings to justify his existence.

If a child is born to over-dogmatic parents, and heavy restraints are placed upon him as to rigid religious disciplines, he has lived a bigot's life in some former life. On reaching adulthood, he is usually saturated with his childhood oppressions; however, his innate hunger for a religious life will move him from one faith to another. In time, the answer for such a person will be that he undergo at first hand some moving or stirring religious experience.

Whatever parents instill into a child regarding God nourishes what the child has remembered of God from his former lives. If a person left the world uncontrite as to his errors in the just previous life, he will look upon God in the early years of this life as a God of punishment. His love for his parents will be tinged with fear; and he will see his parents as reprimanders and punishers.

The true reflection of a child's just previous life is more apparent in the first seven years than any other period of life. Pure, devoted parents intuit this reflection, and tenderly strive to bring forth and reproduce the higher potential within the character and temperament of the child. Thus, the most vital time for love in the parental direction in child training and guidance is within the first seven years of the child's life. During these malleable years of the child, the parents may do their greatest work. When parents fail in their reverent care for a child, the child is placed too soon upon his own resources and yet unformed judgments. In this, the child may become untruthful, insecure, misbehaved.

Whatever is experienced between parents

FIRST ETHERIC CYCLE 19

and child in the first etheric cycle is imprinted upon the child as a pattern of conduct, affecting his attitudes toward the world for the complete lifetime. If a child is given religious or spiritual training in these delicate and impressionable years, this training will be etched and moulded into him. If the parents are prejudiced as to religion, the child must cope with these prejudices for the remainder of his life.

At birth the umbilical cord between the mother and child is replaced by an *etheric cord*. This etheric cord between mother and child enables the mother to have an extreme sensitivity and alertness to the child's needs, and also enables the child to absorb the mother's love and protection. Under normal and happy circumstances, the child is released from the etheric cord between him and his mother in his seventh year—even as he was released from the umbilical cord at birth. However, if there is a heavy pattern of debt overshadowing the mother and child from former lives, the etheric cord between them is painfully accentuated rather than released during the child's seventh year. Thus the etheric cord remains as a weblike enclosure, creating a situation of possessivism. Invariably, one or the other becomes overly attached and dependent, until the debt is resolved. Sometimes this debt extends beyond the present life into future lives.

The spiritual world and the physical world are as one to a child in the first etheric cycle. The child is unstartled by the presence of the angels, and takes the protection of the angels for granted. In some instances a child is more at home with the world of the angels than the world of adults.

> *"Take heed that ye despise not one of these little ones; for I say unto you, That in heaven their angels do always behold the face of my Father which is in heaven."*
> —St. Matthew 18:10

Many of the terrors and fears in childhood are increased by parents who ruthlessly deny a child's assertion that there are angels and that he has seen them. Inasmuch as the child accepts his parents' authority, the child's knowledge of the angels is often nullified. In

FIRST ETHERIC CYCLE 21

this, the child loses a great measure of that comfort and protection which he would otherwise receive from the angels. When the physical parents stand between the child and the protection of the angels, the child's evolvement is left entirely to the responsibility of the parents.

Parents who think of the angels as part of fable or myth always reprove their children for speaking of the angels. If one has denied the reality of the angels in former lives, he will respond to his parents' reproving with a feeling of guilt. When he finally becomes absorbed by an incredulous adult world, he will forget his experiences with the angels.

If one of high evolvement is born to parents who prefer to deny the angels, the child has an inherent intuition to withhold from the parents his knowledge of the angels; thus he is not subjected to their displeasures or reprovings concerning the angels. The child, while yet obedient to the supervision of the parents, is inwardly independent of them and retains a reserve and wisdom concerning all that spiritually occurs to him. Such a child draws upon the moral strength of his former lives and, therefore, complies naturally with the greater rules of life.

When parents reaffirm to their children the reality of the angels, the children turn trustingly to the love and protection of the angels during sickness, fear, and new experiences. The ascertaining of the angels is especially helpful and comforting to children who experience the heartbreak which inevitably comes in the transition between the imaginative years and the adult world.

If a child is physically separated from his mother at birth, the child is protected by the angels. However, if the physical mother loves her child, she may visit the child etherically in dream experience and comfort the child. If a child is adopted and placed in a home of love, the child will have had in a former life some parental experience with those who now would give of themselves that he be cherished and loved. If a child is separated from a loving mother by death, the child is telepathically comforted, overshadowed and protected by his mother in the higher worlds.

FIRST ETHERIC CYCLE

Grace earned in the former or previous life may enable a child to express an unfulfilled or unfinished talent of genius before the child reaches the seventh year. If the former life genius has been unfulfilled, the child will extend and express the genius talent for the complete life. However, if it is but the coloring or overflowing of the genius talent from a former life, the child will express briefly in a prodigy fashion and will cease to express the talent on reaching puberty.

THE LESSER ETHERIC BODY

Even as a seed contains a microscopic image of the plant-to-be, the heart of each person contains a miniature, etheric image of what he has been in former lives and what he may become in the present life. During the first etheric cycle, that is, from birth to the 7th year, the child expands this etheric image into a filmlike replica of his physical body-to-be. The filmlike replica of the physical body is called the *lesser etheric body*.*

*The lesser etheric body dies when the physical body dies. However, there is also a *higher etheric body* which never dies. The higher etheric body, called the everlasting body, is the body with which one travels in dreams, and is the body one inhabits between death and birth. When the lesser etheric body is dissolved at death, it imprints upon one of the immortal atoms of the higher etheric body the complete story of the mental, emotional, and physical actions of the life just lived on earth. These former actions help to determine the shape, size, and appearance of the physical body, and also the emotional tendencies and mental aptitudes in the forthcoming life.

The lesser etheric body acts as a mirror to reflect the actions, emotions, and thoughts of former lives and the present life. The lesser etheric body is also the body of energy, animation, and vitality. From the time of birth to the 7th year of life, the lesser etheric body of a child rapidly increases its size until it reaches adult stature. This accounts for the extreme vitality of children.

The lesser etheric body permeates and saturates the blood stream, the cells, the muscles, and the nerves; it is particularly active in the brain at the base of the skull. A child produces a healthy lesser etheric body if the physical, emotional, and mental actions of former lives have been of pure intent and motive. Imbalanced organs and deformities at birth, and all tendencies to negative habits beginning in infancy and childhood, are reflections of imbalanced actions in former lives which have been imprinted by the soul upon the lesser etheric body. If in former lives there has been an overuse of tension, haste, impatience, or excess in negative habits, a child produces a weakened lesser etheric body of low vitality. A malformed lesser etheric body is due to abuse of the will in former lives. This is reflected into the personality of the child and creates a condition restraining the physical or emotional will.

An untimely cause of death in the former life, such as suicide or death by war, produces a disorganized lesser etheric body in the present life. A child sometimes produces a lesser etheric body saturated with fear due to a frightening death experience in the just previous life.

The many childhood communicable diseases give resiliency and balance to an overly buoyant lesser etheric body, thereby softening and tempering the harsher elements brought through inherited ancestral traits and the just previous life.

During the first etheric cycle the child undergoes a magnification of all events because the developing of the lesser etheric body produces a magnified action. In this period of acute receptivity the child learns to speak by hearing the repetitive sounds around him; he learns to crawl, stand, walk and, finally, to run. All activities around the child are magnified so that he may incorporate the essence of these occurrences and make them part of a familiar world. At the conclusion of the 7th year the lesser etheric body is completely formed, and the period of magnification ends.

SECOND ETHERIC CYCLE

7th Year to 14th Year

The 7th year to the 9th year are the credulous years, the years of mimicry and imagination. During this time a child has more than the intuited memory of former lives to fortify him. He experiences something greater — something soon to be lost in his future adjustment to a demanding world: he relives, inwardly, the remembrance of the world he inhabited just previous to birth. These memories of the life in the pre-birth existence feed his imagination and enable him to intuit the difference between truth and deception. These memories are recalled and relived in the folk tales, fairy tales, and in the imaginative games so much a part of a child's life.

From the 7th year to the 9th year a child creates his world as *he* wishes it. Any imposed suggestion is interpreted by him as an intrusion. If there is a negative or unpleasant condition in his environment, he refuses to incorporate it into his nature and temperament. The imaginative faculty received from his communion with the higher worlds enables him to be free from the external impressions of his environment. In all of his associations in the outer world his forgiving spirit is instantaneous.

Between the 7th year and the 9th year a child may contact an etheric child preparing to re-embody in the world. The etheric child or "invisible playmate" is attracted to the child because of an association with him in some former life. The invisible playmate, being familiar to him, is known by a name and has a distinct identity to the child. The child's association with the etheric playmate is his final uninhibited experience with the higher worlds. Henceforth, any spiritual experience

SECOND ETHERIC CYCLE

he may have later in life will be influenced and colored by comparisons between the physical and spiritual worlds.

When a child plays with dolls from the 1st year to the 7th year, the child is dramatizing the mother's love. When a feminine child plays with dolls from the 7th year to the 9th year, the creative process of her imagination is preparing her for the time she will become a mother of children. The creative process of a male child's imagination inclines him toward mechanical objects, toys and games of action, which condition him for the masculine challenges of life.

The 9th year begins the competitive years. As the child progresses toward the years of puberty, he may become less certain of the infallibility of parents, teachers, and the adult world. If there were prejudiced actions in former lives, the child will have the tendency to be jealous and to hold aversions and dislikes.

In the first stages of puberty the emotional world of a child is a tumultuous reflection of the emotions of past lives; the emotions, instincts, and thoughts inherited from ancestors; the pressure of glandular development; and a budding and approaching individuality. The child has so many pressures brought to bear from so many directions, inwardly and outwardly, that he may often appear absent-minded, dreamlike, or indifferent. In this period the child may also swing the emotional pendulum. The formerly open disposition of a loving child may become introvert and secretive. Such a child is expressing an inner exploring so as to establish certain moods in the temperament. A child who expresses an extrovert nature in the puberty years becomes noisy and boisterous so that he may be less sensitive to the voice of his debts from former lives.

The developing of the glandular system enables a child to experience the ancestral pictures he has inherited through the blood streams of his mother and father. These ancestral pictures, reflecting the virtues and also the errors of his ancestors, move through the glands, blood stream, and consciousness of the child and produce a battleground in him during glandular development. The inner turmoil caused by the inherited pictures of good and negation (1) colors his thoughts, emotions, and actions; (2) induces the budding of his own individuality; (3) gives him a strong instinct for self-preservation; and (4) provides him with a native intelligence.

During the period in which the maternal and paternal ancestral pictures are experienced by the child, he is exposed to the cross currents of the converging ancestral streams. His inner integrity from previous lives must come to grips with the antipathies of the two family lines. These antipathies relate to the conflicts between in-laws, the differences in blood chemistry, the tribal, racial, national, religious, and personal attitudes and prejudices. At this time the child is given the opportunity to overcome any inherited eccentric traits.

If there was little or no tension in the etheric cord between mother and child in the first etheric cycle, the maternal ancestral pictures were absorbed into the child's lesser etheric body in the pre-puberty years. On entering puberty such a child will experience the maternal ancestral pictures indirectly, and the paternal ancestral pictures directly. However, if there was tension in the etheric cord between the mother and child in the first etheric cycle, the child, during puberty, will experience the pictures of both ancestral streams directly. If the child does not have access to his own inner resources and moral strength from former lives, these ancestral pictures will overwhelm him; and he will become a problem to himself and his family.

If the maternal or paternal ancestral pictures are impure, sensuous, and unloving, the child will feel uncomfortable with, and sometimes openly resent, the parent and the parent's blood relatives of that ancestral line.

Between the 12th year and the 14th year a sensitive child intuits which parent held the purest degree of reverence and love during the time of the child's conception. This is the reason why a child is sometimes partial toward one parent. The child may also feel a preference for one parent more than the other due to a loving association with that parent in a previous life. If the mother resented pregnancy, and the child was unwanted by her, or if there was some unhappy relationship between the mother and child in previous lives, the child will resent the discipline given by the mother in his precarious puberty years.

If there was bitter rivalry between the father and son in previous lives, this rivalry may be recapitulated between them during the son's period of paternal ancestral absorption and puberty pressure, thereby creating inharmony and discord within the home.

The ripening glandular system enables one to prepare for future propagation, and also makes it possible for him to begin to align himself with his thought process from former lives. In this, his thoughts begin to be individualistic; and he thinks of himself more as a person than a child. This is the reason why some children, between the ages of 12 and 14, resent their parents' authority and think their parents to be unwise or unknowing.

A highly evolved child, having produced a loving and wholesome individuality in former lives, moves through the second etheric cycle with poise and balance. The child understands the sacredness of close relationships; and he is thankful to those who have given birth to his physical body. He reveres and honors his father and mother.

From the 12th year to the 14th year some children experience a transient religious conversion due to religious zeal in former lives. However, if a child enters into any form of overzealous religious expression of an ecstatic nature, he has the danger of producing a psychic capacity. This will cause a lesion to occur in the lesser etheric body, and the child will prove emotionally unstable for the remainder of life. Precocious psychic functions in puberty are due to former life abuse of spiritual law.

The religious inclinations from former lives may enter a child as a desire for religious experience. A child may also become temporarily prophetic and have unusual and prophetic dreams. During this brief phase of prophecy he will express an exceptional foresight and insight.

SECOND ETHERIC CYCLE

If a child has the misfortune to have little or no religious training, he turns his worship and adoration to things or persons unworthy of his devotion; or he seeks to emulate some prominent or famous personality in the world.

Some children are born today as misfits in society. In former lives they were reckless and irresponsible persons who lived in countries where there is a prevalence of wars and revolutions. In puberty and adolescence these children refuse to conform to the proven standards of the world, and are blind to the advantages around them. From these come the extreme or severe juvenile problems. Parents who have deserted or seriously neglected their children in former lives attract wayward children in this life. In this, they are given the opportunity to fulfill their responsibilities in parenthood. If a wayward child is born to gentle and unassuming parents, the parents have dedicated to try to inspire the child to believe in good and a better way of life. There is, however, a majority of children being born who enter the world blessed by the greater attributes of grace. These children are qualified to contribute to science, healing, education, art, music, literature, and religion. From such children comes the hope for the world's future.

THIRD ETHERIC CYCLE

14th Year to 21st Year

The 14th year to the 17th year is the time any remaining remnants of ancient tribal memories and compulsions are reflected onto the emotions. This is the time young people may be attracted to atavistic music with primitive rhythm. Music of the accentuated jazz variety aids in the releasing of primitive congestions pressing upon the base of the skull, wherein are reflected the tribal and atavistic compulsions. It is normal and healthy that youth experience this freeing of atavistic energy. The parents of these young people should strive to look upon such primitive antics with as much charitableness as possible, remembering their own adolescent pressures, so that this period of association between parents and children will carry no lasting, regretful memories. If parents use shortsighted disciplines upon a son or daughter, these atavistic aggressions may turn inward rather than outward, and the adolescent will become acutely self-conscious, timid, and insecure.

Young people are sometimes attracted to folk music. Folk music helps them to bring forth the reflected memories of former lives' national customs and conscience.

The period of adolescence is a chimera of emotions, revealing the primitive aggressions of the youth. In this period a boy or girl may move from one fad to another. Fads, slang phrases, and cliques are part of the memory from ancient tribal ceremonial habits, attitudes, and customs. The attitude of absolute acceptance or rejection of individuals or things stems from clan instinctual memory.

In the period of the 14th year to the 17th year a young person may enter into a period of haste; of impatience against time. He feels he is adult, responsible, and mature. And he feels the overpowering compulsion to speed up the processes of life. He may begin to experiment with sound and speed. Sound expresses the intensity of his emotions; speed fulfills the need to express his will.

Art expressed in the adolescent years carries daring, beauty, and originality. The emotions of young people at this time may reflect the creative worlds. In this, they present new ideas in art — ideas which are in advance of the time. Such art is a combined action of talents from former lives and that which the soul is seeking to speak through color, object, and form.

The impulse of one's will, and the degree of the will, may be seen between the 14th year and the 17th year. The will of the boy or girl is indicative of the soul's capacity, the traits of character, the quality of temperament, and the type of personality to be expressed in the present life. A young person, highly evolved from previous lives, will manifest in his 14th year to 17th year a mature conscience with the faculty to judge between right and wrong. However, if a youth reflects a cunning will from a previous life, he will enter the world seeking to manipulate the wills of others. Over-aggression, between the 14th year and the 17th year, stems from primitive impulses of former ages, and is also a direct reflection of previous lives of forcefulness. A boy or girl with more than average self-control has tempered the will in previous lives.

If a young person is highly evolved as to his will, emotions, and thoughts, he begins from the 17th year onward to steadily withdraw from the primitive, ancestral compulsions; and moves more directly toward a concentrated focus upon the individuality to be expressed in this life. Engrossed in the creating of individuality, he may temporarily move out of sympathetic alignment with those in his own environment and with others in the world. He sometimes withdraws from parental influence, feeling more adequate than his parents, and becoming a critic as to their way of life.

In rare instances a decided emphasis of grace may be expressed by young persons within these formative years. This appears as genius talent, insight, and a capacity to think with maturity and clarity. Such young people enter the world to fulfill something greater than ancestral reflection. Among these are to be found the future greater scientists, noble statesmen, outstanding craftsmen, dedicated artisans, and brilliant composers of melodic music.

It is unusual when one moves through an uneventful puberty and adolescence. Only many harmonious actions of former lives will produce an individual who emerges from childhood to manhood with ease and poise.

The 18th year to the 21st year are the agnostic years. The young man or woman, approaching a budding intellect, begins to analyze and weigh the reality and tangibility of God. In this period there is the danger of losing the thread of belief in God, and becoming atheistic for the complete life. This is the period in which one must transpose his parents' help and supervision to the belief in God's help and provision. When there is an extreme egotism and a deliberate cultivation of the agnostic attitude, one is less likely to have access to the memories of talents and vocations of previous lives; and, he is thus more likely to make wrong choice in vocation.

These years in which the young person becomes aware that he must begin to shift for himself, either to earn a livelihood or to make right choice as to how to earn a livelihood, may be painful years of indecision as to education, vocation, and placement. A conscientious young man or woman, overshadowed by the desire to please parents and those near by, may find it difficult to express individual choice and also conform to parental expectations. It is on the whole a trying period previous to maturity.

If the individual has devoted himself to religion in an ascetic manner in a former life, he will undergo much analysis of religion in his 18th year to 21st year. If he has suffered religious persecution in a previous life, he will avoid church-going. If he has had previous lives of stamina, and faith in God, he will survive this agnostic time through a stalwart knowing — a form of knowing between intuition and faith.

FOURTH ETHERIC CYCLE

21st Year to 28th Year

An etheric cycle is a tide of life occurring in regular seven-year intervals. Each etheric cycle presents a combination of the grace of good works from former lives and also the unfinished actions, unexpressed ambitions, and unfulfilled qualities from previous lives. Each etheric cycle gives one the opportunity to renew the action of grace and to give birth to a nobler self. Every seven years the grace within the soul's record seeks to return something Godlike to man. Thus, a lesson unabsorbed in one etheric cycle will repeat itself with more urgency in a coming etheric cycle.

The Godlike, or spiritual, in man is presented through his actions as an ethic or principle. The soul emanates this ethic as quality. The thought projects the ethic as a pure, interpreting attribute. The emotions activate the ethic as the love motive or intent. When there is a freeing of the ethic through thought and emotions, there is a rare participation in life, either through some genius action or some outstanding achievement and accomplishment.

The conscience is the voice of the ethic. When a person fails to release his ethic, he fails to receive what his conscience would say to him; and, therefore, he very often acts with a shortsightedness detrimental to himself and harmful to others. When the ethic and conscience work together, one has a divine ballast, or spiritual equilibrium, which holds him firmly to the moral purpose within his conduct. When the ethic and the conscience are in perfect accord, the soul is free to expand its action.

The lessons learned through many and repeated experiences in former lives develop the inherent faculties or the common sense attributes. When these inherent faculties are blended with the soul-faculties, the ethic is unrestrained.

FOURTH ETHERIC CYCLE

From the 21st year to the 24th year the ethic may be discerned by either its presence or its absence. During this period the life course is charted. One's use or abuse of the ethic determines whether or not he will be a responsible or irresponsible person in life.

The fourth etheric cycle, that is, the 21st year to the 28th year, seeks to establish the personality. In this cycle one has the opportunity to incorporate and blend the personalities of former lives with the present personality. One is either a repelling or an attracting personality to others. The attracting element in personality is acquired from many ethical personalities of former lives. A repelling personality is the result of many hypocritical, deceptive, and untrustworthy personalities of previous lives.

If there are any lingering vanities and conceits from personalities of past lives, these are expressed in this etheric cycle as egotism and self-importance. When one has the feeling of superiority and self-importance, he may be placed in situations where others instantaneously trust him; but he will fail to fulfill their expectations. However, if a person has lived within his ethic in former personalities, he will liberate his ethic between the 21st year and 28th year. This will manifest as reliability and integrity.

In the fourth etheric cycle it may be seen whether or not one brings with him certain grace or inclination toward original talents, or whether he prefers to conform to that expected of him as to proven grooves or patterns set up by family or friends. Personality will also indicate whether there is a weak or strong will tendency toward persistence, consistency, and stamina.

The fourth etheric cycle offers to one the opportunity to make selective choice or decision between family attachments, marriage, the bearing of children, vocation, talents. All of these will direct themselves to his attention repeatedly, and vitally concern him. During this period his paramount interest and choice will influence, to a great degree, the range of action within the personality of this life. The choice of vocation, when individualistic, reflects the soul's record of creative and original expression in former lives. If one dedicates himself to the welfare of mankind, he has in past lives opened his heart to the needs of men; and he comes to the world that he may serve.

If one is harmoniously centered within his personality in his 21st year, he will no longer resemble his parents or grandparents as to physical appearance. Former life traits and characteristics will begin to influence his appearance; and he will emerge fully individualized, expressing a distinct personality.

At the age of 21, one begins for the first time to assume direct responsibility for his feelings and thoughts. He also begins to absorb the essence of his responsible or irresponsible actions of former lives. If he is self-reliant, his sense of responsibility will be clarified concerning marriage, thoughts of marriage, work, and vocation.

Marriage relationships in former lives affect one's attitude toward marriage in the present life. If a person has lived for many lives close to the race or tribal propagation ideal — or that is, marriage being arranged by parents — he will marry to please his parents rather than listen to the dictates of his heart. If a person fails to align himself with his emotional grace, his choice and selection of a mate will be influenced solely by biological and physical attraction. If in former lives he has established reverence for the marriage state, he is more likely to select his mate with pure love. However, regardless of one's maturity or immaturity, the grace within the soul's record of former lives may precipitate a catalyst recognition of the true mate.

If one enters into serious parental conflicts in this time of his life, this indicates that in just previous lives he has failed to fulfill certain obligations to family. If one finds himself in family relationships which stand between him and his choice in marriage, vocation, or religion — and if this is but a temporary situation and resolvable — the person in this etheric cycle will be balancing some former life's unfinished action. However, if he finds himself in a fixed or unyielding condition, in which he is faced seemingly for life with persons who stand between him and his free-

FOURTH ETHERIC CYCLE

dom of choice in selection of a marriage partner, vocation, religion, or the fulfilling of some talent — he will then be in the process of paying a debt yet unresolved from a former life.

If one enters his 24th year with the belief that personality is the only and all-important expression, he will limit himself to personal satisfaction through sensation and experimentation. However, if he has the grace to eradicate or eliminate any remaining conceits or egotism, he will undergo a deflationary process, which will enable him to achieve a sense of values to equal his sense of responsibility. And between the 24th year and the 28th year he will begin to develop a more philosophical outlook as to his world, and come to recognize that there are other forces at work shaping his destiny. Thus, he will enter into more charitable viewpoints.

If a person is unimpressionable, or drifts aimlessly through this important period in his life, he shall cease to evolve beyond personality and its external action. Thus, many people remain crystallized in personality expression alone, for they fail to move with the tide of the fourth etheric cycle. Such men and women remain emotionally and mentally immature for their complete lives.

Because the 21st year to the 28th year is a period of personality absorption, only in rare instances is there the seeking of religious experience. However, if there has been a previous life of pure faith, the person will respect the rights of others and will also have a reverence for the right of others to worship. And if there has been spiritual expression in a former life, the person will manifest a higher degree of grace, and thus become aware of spiritual laws and the spiritual worlds.

FIFTH ETHERIC CYCLE

28th Year to 35th Year

The fourth etheric cycle placed the individual in an adult world; the fifth etheric cycle relates him to a mature world. In these years one enters into mature obligations, and seeks to live up to the mature standards and expectations of others. There is a tendency for a person to express an exaggerated sense of self-assurance between the 28th year and the 35th year. If one brings emotional or mental immaturity from a former life, he will develop set convictions and lifelong prejudices. If a person is in accord with the aspects of grace from his former lives, he will benefit by the maturing process in this etheric cycle and establish a perspective and foresight toward the forthcoming events in his life.

Because the will of the individual begins

a more maturing expression in the fifth etheric cycle, he will have certain trials and temptations placed before him. These trials pertain to marriage, religion, occupation, and talents. All of the trials experienced until the 33rd year build steadily toward a number of crucial, inward trials between the 33rd year and the 35th year. In some instances major, spiritual trials occur in one or more facets of self-revealing. Severe trials may manifest in (1) the marriage relationship, (2) one's faith in religion, (3) the vocational and working environment, and (4) the creative aptitudes. During this period one may experience a deep religious longing; and he may be filled with a restless yearning to create.

The trials pertaining to vocation and occupation determine the degree of authority a person will have in this life and how the authority will be used. If in some former life one has earned a place in society through effort and struggle, he will begin to reap this as grace in his 33rd year to 35th year. His abilities will be singled out. And he will receive promotion or advancement in working environment; or he will be placed in a position of authority. From this will come the opportunity to free certain power attributes from former lives. However, if a person has used funds or monies in a careless manner in a past life, or if he has pinched pennies in a miserly fashion in a past life, he will be placed in working environments where he will receive little recognition and no rewards.

The 28th year to the 35th year is the migratory period of life. The migratory impulse at this time often causes certain events to arise which change the normal course of action, thereby influencing men and women to establish themselves in distant or new places. Parental associations, which formerly were comforting, may become hampering and stifling. Those who are more individualistic will seek to be detached from these reminders of dependency, and to go where they will be recognized as to what they feel and know they are.

In marriage one assumes the former life debts of the marriage partner, and thus accelerates the process of balancing the imbalanced actions from former lives. If one has sullied or abused the marriage vows in a previous life, he or she inevitably attracts a mate with little or no reverence for the procreative act and for the marriage bond. In this, one will experience extremely painful lessons in the marriage trials between the 28th year and the 35th year.

During the marriage trials in the fifth etheric cycle, the sexual-will dominates the glandular system. One who has an aggressive nature may enter into an unlicensed sexual experimental phase. If one is inclined to be intellectual and analytical, he may enter into a period of rebellion regarding the marriage burdens and responsibilities he has assumed. Such a person may think that life asks too much from him. If the emotions are predominant, and one is more mystically inclined, he will sentimentalize his relationships with immature expectations; and he will weigh down his marriage partner with infantile concepts as to what he thinks marriage is. The mature standards of the fifth etheric cycle are beyond the capacity of persons who are devoted wholly to self and self-experience.

FIFTH ETHERIC CYCLE

Those who fail to enter into maturity in the fifth etheric cycle make poor providers and neglectful parents. However, if two persons have set up the ideal rhythm in marriage in former lives, marriage in this etheric cycle will become the highest union; and the marriage partners will blend and fuse their previous life association into a successful relationship. Children produced from such a union make up the ideal family.

From the 28th year to the 35th year one comes into moral responsibility for his actions and appetites. If he develops any negative appetites or selfish habits, such as vulgarity in speech, dishonesty, adultery, or the excessive use of drugs, alcohol, or tobacco — these will produce *etheric scars* which may remain for life. If these appetites and habits are not resolved before the 35th year, they are carried over into the next life and will appear as certain defects and weaknesses. However, if one becomes discontented and contrite as to these habits and actions, he will have the opportunity to resolve them in this life.

If a person shows the promise of a great

talent he has inherited from former lives, he undergoes a talent trial in the fifth etheric cycle. This trial pertains to whether or not he rejects his talent, compromises and commercializes his talent, or expresses the aesthetic meaning within the creative experience. His decision as to how he uses or abuses his talent will determine his peace of mind for the complete life.

If one has created selflessly in a former life, such selfless actions will provide him with the training and opportunity to qualify his works of creation in the present life. However, if one has used his talent or talents in an egotistical or conceited fashion in a previous life, regardless of his qualifications, he will receive little or no recognition for his talents in this life.

Certain persons undergo a de-glamorizing process between the 33rd year and the 35th year. For example, one may lose his or her employment more than once so as to reproportion the mental outlook. In marriage one may suffer some disillusionment concerning the marriage partner. During these years one may also lose something of self-assurance pertaining to the ability to fulfill tasks in the home and in the business world. This de-glamorizing process often produces a yearning or need for spiritual comfort and a closer relating to God.

Everyone has the opportunity for the *Shadow of God* to fall upon him between the 33rd year and the 35th year. During this period the germinal quality of the soul, that is, the everlasting life inherent in each person, is activated. Each one's individual evolvement determines how this germinal action will manifest; for to each man and woman this is a unique, personalized experience. Those who are atheistic begin an inner battle or contest with certain unfamiliar levels of soul-action. In this period, atheistic or agnostic persons are very close to recognizing and acknowledging that there is a Plan, an Intelligence, a Justice. However, these persons will need many lives before the *Shadow of God* becomes the reality.

Those who are emotionally immature will react to the spiritual trials of the fifth etheric cycle with a mystical attitude. Those who are intellectually inclined will delve into comparative facets of religion. Others will find in formal worships the background for their religious lives. Those who have lived spiritually in former lives will recapitulate a relating to the spiritual worlds. Thus, they will undergo an illuminative experience through which the grace earned from sacrifice and pure works in former lives will produce certain spiritual powers. Such inspired persons will henceforth live dedicated spiritual lives, giving their loving helps to the world.

From the 33rd year to the 35th year something deep within — between man and soul, soul and God — presses forth and seeks to be heard. These are the years of the two paths: one path represents the materialistic way of life; the other path relates to a higher way of life. A person chooses to serve the idols of man, or to serve the Will of God.

If one has had spiritual understanding in previous lives, a blessing will appear in the latter part of the fifth etheric cycle. This blessing sometimes manifests in the form of a sacred book, the spiritual teacher, or one or more spiritual gifts. And, one who has spiritual grace from previous lives will make a lifetime alignment with God.

SIXTH ETHERIC CYCLE

35th Year to 42nd Year

Man is more than the result of biological passion. He is more than the influence of a gene. He is a spiritual being speaking through a soul. There are periods when man obscures this truth, and periods when he reclaims it. Each life gives man the opportunity to recover something of the spiritual man within, and to return to the spiritual state while living in the physical world.

It is God's design that man in each life extend his consciousness and increase his capacity to love. The skills expressed by man from life to life are but temporary alliances to enable him to master a certain degree of will and thought, so that he may attain the ability to create immortal works. When selfless love is the theme from life to life, one is enabled

SIXTH ETHERIC CYCLE

to live all lives purposefully, harmoniously, creatively. Love is the key to the world of man and the key to the World of God.

Many persons disclaim the law of re-embodiment because the solemn side of justice, or the payment of self-accumulated debts, is depressing to them. Until each person comes into perfect accord with his soul, he is in a state of perpetual indebtedness to some one or some thing. Love for one another is the beginning of resolving this indebtedness.

There is a difference between an intellectual belief in the law of reincarnation and the heart's intuition of the law of re-embodiment. When one has the heart's intuition of the law of re-embodiment, he enters the world as a giver; for he knows that he has access to eternal substance and eternal life, and that he may give all he is and still retain what he is. The greater personages either know or intuit the law of re-embodiment. Illumined and selfless poets, composers, sculptors, and artists devote their talents to portraying the eternal existence of man.

From the 35th year until the time of death

all persons relate themselves more intimately and directly with their souls. When one has had the grace to respond rhythmically to the draughts of remembrance during the first five etheric cycles, he will enter into the productive years of his life with the means of rendering some lasting good for the world. When one, through rebellion and resistance, has failed to coordinate with the absorption periods of the first five etheric cycles, he will enter into a struggle with his unruly emotions and yet undisciplined mind; and he will find his actions centered within a battleground of life. Thus, he will be little qualified to channel the good earned in this life, or to reap the harvest of former lives.

Each one comes to the world to give something of himself. And each one retains his record, not only in his soul, but he leaves the record of his works upon the lives of others. The crises, pressures, and struggles, which begin in the sixth etheric cycle, are the means through which one is squeezed, pressed, and pushed, so that he may leave a mark upon the world. Some persons prefer to leave a

SIXTH ETHERIC CYCLE 63

mark of pain or evil, rather than that which God would have them give to the world. The unceasing commands of the soul, and the continued demands of the outer world enable one who has utilized the spiritual impetus of the fifth etheric cycle to extract the essence of good works from former lives, and to activate the unique genius of the present life. In this, he will leave to the world something essentially original and creative; a golden wondrousness which only he can produce. When one has failed to move upward with the spiritual impetus of the fifth etheric cycle, he faces the danger of a decline as to his efforts and achievements. However, he has the opportunity throughout his life to respond to his higher nature, if he will; and thus leave a mark of good upon the earth.

In the 35th year each one begins to prepare for his future embodiment. His food habits and appetites, the care of his physical body, his appreciation of the good and the beautiful, his reverence towards love, his philosophical and spiritual outlook, create not only the day by day comfort, convenience, and peace of mind, but they also create the pattern for the next life.

When one reaches the 35th year, the lesser etheric body begins to reduce in size. The tissues of the flesh begin to be loosened; the muscles begin to slacken; the organs are less responsive. And the physical body begins its first appearance of aging. Over the years, one gradually loses certain animation and vitality within the lesser etheric body. Were it not for the lesser etheric body's shrinking or decreasing, an adult's appearance would remain youthful throughout life. As the lesser etheric body decreases, the unresolved emotions and thoughts, photographed upon the lesser etheric body, become more prominent in the external expression of the emotions and thoughts. The lesser etheric body continues to decrease in size from the 35th year until death.

SEVENTH ETHERIC CYCLE

42nd Year to 49th Year

The moral conflicts and chastity challenges during the seventh etheric cycle, when met and mastered, produce the moral stamina for the next life. If one accomplishes a victory over the senses, he builds the grace for a pure, chaste and reverent life in the coming embodiment.

The true creative impulse seeks to penetrate the heart and the brain from the 42nd year onward. In the 42nd year, the glands which furnish the racial procreation impulses begin to withdraw their influence from the thinking process, so that one's thoughts may become more exposed to the creative power of the soul. In this, the glands begin to play more heavily upon the emotions. If one has dominance over his moral actions, he experiences this period of glandular transition with understanding; and the splendid valor of the soul's strength moves into him.

Many people wreck their personal lives between the 42nd year and the 49th year because they are unable to interpret the glandular transition taking place within the senses, emotions, and thoughts. If one prefers to respond more to his sensual desires rather than to the creative power of the soul, he will undergo tremendous emotional and mental upheavals.

The former life's reverent or irreverent attitudes toward procreation are recapitulated in the seventh etheric cycle. If prudery has been expressed in the previous life or in the present life, the person may spend his passions in an unbridled and licentious manner during the seventh etheric cycle. When the procreative urges are used licentiously in this period, the result is tragedy, sorrow, unhappiness, bitterness. And, in the 49th year the person will begin a severe dissolution process relating to his egotism and self-will.

In the 14th year, when the glands develop,

the debts from former lives are as a storm brewing in the senses. In the 42nd year, the glands are in the midst of the tempest or storm. Some people become so engulfed in this storm that the rational thought process is swept away, especially if they have in some manner profaned the procreation impulses in former lives or in the present life.

Even though one has fulfilled all the rules for health, he may begin in the seventh etheric cycle to place an emotional and mental emphasis upon health factors. If the 42nd year presents a climax in health, this is due to previous life abuse of the laws governing the physical body.

In the seventh etheric cycle one may produce some artistic or creative talent of daring. Thus ripe genius may come forth, reflecting familiar talents from former lives. Genius appearing in the seventh etheric cycle is dissimilar to the genius which sometimes appears in the earlier years of childhood. Genius during childhood is usually an overflow from former-life genius and, therefore, is more often unlasting or transient. Genius appearing between the 42nd year and the 49th year is of a lasting nature. Such genius is a combined state of the ripening events of this life and the talents of former lives, and it comes to give something to the world rather than as an expression of temperament and personality.

EIGHTH ETHERIC CYCLE

49th Year to 56th Year

A man is born to a world of wonder in the 7th year, amazement in the 14th year, responsibility in the 21st year, direct action in the 28th year, the spiritual in the 35th year, his moral debts in the 42nd year, and his conscience in the 49th year. If one has failed to meet the soul's requirements in the previous etheric cycles, and fails to accept that which his conscience would speak or reveal, he must await another life and timing to expiate the erroneous acts of the present life.

It may be observed that more life patterns are changed in the eighth etheric cycle than in any other period of life. In this etheric cycle one may seek to overthrow his home environment and family responsibility, for conscience, when limited by selfishness, works in a distorted manner. Such action invokes a heavy penalty. Thus, many self-willed persons increase rather than resolve their debts during this time. Those who take their happiness at the expense of others less strong always live under the shadow of their own guilts.

All selfish and self-centered actions are photographed etherically upon the lesser etheric body. In time, these form an *egotistical shell*. If one has been wholly absorbed in the pursuit of material advantage or gain, this egotistical shell turns inward in the 49th year and is felt as pain, remorse. The 49th year to the 56th year are the years of retribution and egotistical dissolution; for the previous actions of arrogance, thoughtlessness, self-importance, self-centeredness, are searched by the heart and the soul. Men, more than women, suffer in the eighth etheric cycle. However, if a woman has some tendency towards a masculine mentality, she will also experience a period of self-deflation.

When one has lived conscientiously, he will find the compensation years in the eighth etheric cycle. Having served selflessly without thought of reward, he will reap the good of these retributive years. And some men and women rise to the extreme height as to their merit, achievement, and skill.

NINTH ETHERIC CYCLE

56th Year to 63rd Year

The ninth etheric cycle is the wisdom cycle. During this period a person has the opportunity to prove whether he is charitable or tyrannical. One who is strongly patriarchal or matriarchal is likely to assume a tyrannical authority, and to impose his or her traditions upon relatives and friends. A magnanimous person, absorbed by cultural and humanitarian interests, looks upon the various members of his family as individuals, retaining his own individuality and perspective as to the sacred meaning of close relationships. His counsel and his wisdom make him a welcome and revered participant in the actions of his family and friends.

In the ninth etheric cycle some persons, who have command of possessions, will dom-

NINTH ETHERIC CYCLE

inate their loved ones. Their feelings of power through possessions will color all relationships; and they would seek to retain their possessions even beyond the gates of death. Such persons re-embody with grasping and greedy hearts, and often find themselves in environments which take much from them and return less.

Those who have failed to live through their own efforts and achievements are likely to feel in the ninth etheric cycle that they should be supported by their children or society. These persons, who prefer to live through family or descendents, often reflect ungrateful and parasitical attitudes. In coming lives they enter the world with hardships, handicaps, and heavy disciplines.

Those who have adhered to both honor and earning will assert themselves to remain independent in the ninth etheric cycle. It is possible in this period for such persons to produce a remarkable renascence in ability and expression. And in the forthcoming lives they shall be competent, capable — and will enter the world prepared for authority.

If one has used his body as a temple for God, he shall reap the rewards of health and inner peace during the ninth etheric cycle. If he has profaned his body in this life or other lives, he will become neurotically aware of his body, of its disintegration; and he will speak incessantly about his various ailments, magnifying and dramatizing them.

In the ninth etheric cycle some people feel compelled to visit countries unfamiliar to them in this life. Such compulsions to travel are activated by an inner, nostalgic memory of lands where they have known former lives of power, pain, joy, love. Their souls direct them to these faraway places so that they may bring some latent remembrance closer to the surface layer of their consciousness and, thus, absorb it into the actions of this life and future lives.

TENTH ETHERIC CYCLE

63rd Year to 70th Year

The tenth etheric cycle is the philosophical cycle. Until the 63rd year, one is an actor in the dramas of life. From the 63rd year onward, he gathers the essence from his past activities, and becomes an observer of the dramas of life. A person, who enters the tenth etheric cycle with passions still demanding obedience from the senses, enters a senility cycle rather than a philosophical cycle. An individual who has lived reverently, lovingly, and peaceably, will experience many blessings in the tenth etheric cycle; the blessings of fruitful comprehension; the blessings of philosophical acceptance; and more — the blessings of being close once again to the heaven worlds. For now, one begins to prepare for the inevitable initiation: Death.

To one who has obtained the philosophical outlook, death is not extinction, but extension. During the 63rd year a person, who holds the belief in a life after death, is prepared by the Angel of Death to face death as a natural transition — something to be walked toward rather than feared. Those who have failed to attain a wholesome and reverent belief in God are unable to become inwardly familiar with the Angel of Death, and thus the fear of death permeates their thoughts and actions.

Previous to the tenth etheric cycle, one has created the pattern for the next life. In the tenth etheric cycle he weaves the design for the next life. One who enters a senility cycle rather than a philosophical cycle, between the 63rd year and the 70th year, is subjected to decaying thoughts' and fears. He is impatient with his environment; his memories are bitter and regretful; and he sometimes estranges himself from loved ones. There may also appear a miserly and parsimonious attitude toward money and possessions, especially if the person has believed in the past years that money was the means of power. What one fears in this life is imprinted upon the heart and soul and, therefore, will become a reality in the next life. Thus, one who, in the latter years, dwells too often on thoughts of poverty will be born in the forthcoming life to parents who are impoverished and poverty-stricken.

When a person enters the philosophical cycle with reverence and a forgiving heart, he shall express harmony and beauty in some manner in the next life. One whose emotions are devoid of fear, hate, and anger shall re-embody with charm, magnanimity and graciousness. And if one has absorbed and retained the higher mental concepts of the age or period in which he lives, he shall possess in his next life the creative faculty of lucid thought.

> *"I am the resurrection, and the life: he that believeth in me, though he were dead, yet shall he live: And whosoever liveth and believeth in me shall never die."*
> —St. John 11:25,26

PART TWO

MANTRAMIC PRAYERS

EMOTIONAL ETHERIC GROOVES

The lesser etheric body is similar to a photographic film in that it imprints and mirrors the actions, emotions, and thoughts of former lives, and of the present life. Unruly emotions of previous lives have engraved and etched arterial or groovelike canals in the lesser etheric body. Arterial or groovelike canals are also formed in the lesser etheric body by passive and fatalistic emotional attitudes and acts over many lives. A person with a heavy emphasis upon the emotional etheric grooves in the lesser etheric body is born to the physical world with either an indecisive will, or a lack of self-control. If he has an indecisive will, he follows the line of least resistance. If he lacks self-control, he is self-destructive, harming himself more than others.

Mantramic prayers are especially helpful in redirecting the contraclockwise currents of the emotional etheric grooves into clockwise or creative currents. In this, mantramic prayers help one to become self-reliant and to express his individual will — and therefore, his own individuality.

MENTAL ETHERIC CLOTS

A person who has been unteachable and mentally inflexible in past lives has formed mental etheric clots in the lesser etheric body. These mental etheric clots are in close proximity to the brain, and sustain the decaying thoughts of former lives. The negative thoughts of this life automatically revolve around, and adhere to, the carbon-like mental etheric clots, restricting the creative aspect of thought in the present life. When a person has an etheric clot, he repeats the same mistakes from life to life without benefit of their lessons. He is in danger of becoming laggard, and thus of being shut away from his creative genius and the higher aspects of his soul.

Mantramic speaking has the power to

dissolve the mental etheric clots in the lesser etheric body. When the mental etheric clots are dissolved, one frees the grace from former lives, and also opens up a mentality expressing his own particular individuality.

THE SPOKEN MANTRAM

The spoken mantram has a vibrational and tonal effect upon the lesser etheric body. Therefore, when the mantram is spoken correctly and regularly, the currents within the emotional etheric grooves are redirected, and the mental etheric clots are dissolved. In time, one may open the grace of his soul, and he will benefit from the reverence and sacrificial grace from former lives. He may begin to assimilate and translate the grace of pure thinking into the thoughts and actions of the present life. And, inevitably, he will see the outer results of his inner transition and change.

A mantramic prayer should be spoken with sincere feeling, uttermost faith, deep reverence, and joyful expectation. With practice, one will discover and discern the lilt or nuance concealed within the mantram; and he will come to recognize the key or catalyst words to the need. When a mantramic prayer is spoken correctly, a warming glow may be felt throughout the emotions, and light will enter the thoughts.

One should select the mantram which is suitable to his need. The words of the mantram should be spoken aloud with firm and modulated tones. If it is inconvenient to speak the mantram due to lack of privacy, it is best to form each word of the mantram upon the lips in soft or muted tones, so that the creative action within speech may fulfill the beneficial intent of the mantram.

A mantramic prayer should not be chanted in a singsong manner. It is important that one avoid dwelling intellectually upon the mantramic prayer while speaking the mantram. To speak a mantramic prayer repetitiously, or in wrong timing, or to delete or change any of the words in the mantramic prayer, will nullify the living vitality contained within the mantram.

The words in a mantramic prayer are com-

MANTRAMIC PRAYERS

bined to fulfill a specific purpose. The formula accompanying each mantram designates the time of the day and the number of days to speak the particular mantram.

There are certain times of the day in which the lesser etheric body is more closely related to the soul: on arising, at 10 a.m., at noon, at 3:30 p.m., at sunset, and before sleep. Thus, the time of the day given in the mantramic formula correlates to the soul's equation and timing.

The rhythm of the soul is determined by the debts and the grace of past lives and the present life. The number of days alloted to the use of a mantram correlates to the rhythm of the soul. A five-day mantram is to bring order to the senses. A ten-day mantram pertains to disciplines, or to chronic conditions. A fifteen-day mantram concerns one's emotions as related to others. A twenty-day mantram is to overcome the negative ancestral traits, and produce a lucid and expressive individuality. A twenty-eight-day mantram is an extended mantramic speaking to modify the debts of former lives, and to receive the grace of clarification. A thirty-day mantram is to build insulation against the antichrist challenges in the world.

MARRIAGE AND THE HOME

1. MANTRAM TO SUSTAIN MARRIAGE GRACE

Speak:—

**My love moves before me,
increasing my patience.
My strength is hewn out
of the rock of God's
strength for me. I fear
not responsibility.**

Read:— Marriage grace and marriage debts from former lives direct the choice of a mate in the present life. To extend the marriage grace from the previous life into the marriage of the present life, marriage should be fulfilled on four levels: (1) the physical, (2) the emotional, (3) the mental, and (4) the spiritual. Marriage requires patience, strength, and a sense of responsibility. When these are observed, reverence will support the physical demands of marriage; love will sustain the emotional needs in the marriage tie; and charitable patience will strengthen the mutual intellectual interests. In time, this will produce a spiritual union, the ultimate goal of marriage.

Formula: Time: On arising, and at sunset
             Days: Twenty-eight

2. MANTRAM TO PROTECT THE HOME

Speak:—

> **May the Guardian Angel of this family protect our home, and help us to share our trials with consideration, love, and peace.**

Read:— Until the Guardian Angel of the family appears, the family environment is but a house or shelter rather than a home. When pure love and dedication are expressed by the members of a family, the Guardian Angel will help to sustain the purity and purpose of the family in the home. The Guardian Angel of the family protects the home from intrusion, and also watches over the welfare of the souls, minds, and bodies within a sacred home.

Formula: Time: Noon
Days: Twenty-eight

3. Mantram for a Dedicated Father

Speak:—

**I am the mind of my home.
I seek to be the honor,
the strength, and the wisdom
of the home. May my sons
and daughters bless and
make more peaceful the earth.**

Read:— The male parent of the home has access to the patriarch aspect of "our Father which art in heaven." The true father sees his offspring as more than the product of his loins, for he knows each child is a sacred responsibility entrusted to him. He prays for wisdom to discipline his children with impartiality. And he assumes fatherhood as a garment of veneration and love. Therefore, his children respect and revere him.

Formula: Time: Sunset
Days: Ten

4. MANTRAM FOR A DEDICATED MOTHER

Speak:—

**I am the heart of my home;
the flame in the hearth.
My grace knows my task, and
my soul directs me.**

Read: A sacred mother is a fountain of life. The prayers of a selfless mother are always answered, for the mother has a communion with the mercy level of the higher worlds. A mother who devotes herself to fulfilling her purpose keeps her home inviolate, pure. She teaches her children certain root ethics of life, and inspires them to share, to love, to serve. So does she, as the heart of the home, kindle the altar flame of the hearth.

Formula: Time: Noon
Days: Twenty-eight

5. Mantram for Domestic or Marital Problem

Speak:—
In my choice there was neither accident nor wrong design. I relate myself to the guidance of my soul, and I shall accept the Will of God.

Read: Choice in marriage is overdirected by the soul. The soul never makes a mistake. The souls of two people, who are united in marriage, work continually to overcome weakness with strength. Marital inharmony is caused by refusal to accept the marital debts of this life and former lives. When there seems no relief to a domestic or marital problem, the husband and wife should blend their prayers and turn to God for the solution. Justice and grace shall enter the marriage; and the tensions and dissensions will be clarified and resolved. However, if one of the members of a marriage fails to understand the spiritual lesson involved in the marriage crisis, the domestic or marital problem may engulf them and destroy the inner kernel of the marriage.

Formula: Time: Noon and sunset
Days: Ten

6. Mantram To Overcome In-Law Intrusion

Speak:—

May this marriage become a sacred marriage of unison, fulfillment, and peace. May our hearts be opened, and our lesser desires be overcome. May the oil of preciousness anoint this union.

Read: The first three years of marriage determine whether the husband and wife retain a dependence upon the strength of their parents, or have any remaining covetousness of their parents' possessions. In the first three years of marriage, the husband and wife must qualify themselves to one another and to the world. If there is any remaining dependence upon one or more parents, this will invite in-law intrusion. The first five years of marriage determine whether the sexual relationship between the husband and wife shall be sensual or reverent. A reverent sexual relationship will cleanse away any remnant of lust from former lives. If both husband and wife have resolved their debts of covetousness and lust from former lives, they will be enabled to resolve in-law intrusion before the ninth year of their marriage. If there still remains in-law dominance and intrusion at the conclusion of nine years of marriage, this indicates the unwillingness of the husband or wife to meet the debts of former lives. Heavy debts are incurred by parents who willfully intrude upon the marital life of their children. Such persons disguise their egotism as maternal or paternal authority. Conflicts caused by in-law intrusion are overcome in only one manner: when the husband and wife have established their dependence upon one another, rather than dependence upon their parents.

Formula: Time: Noon
Days: Ten

7. MANTRAM FOR RECONCILIATION

Speak:—

May our love withstand the storm of circumstance. We fear not the record of the past, and behold the light of a new day. We look within, and begin again with joy.

Read: When a person with an inflexible will is ripe for the marriage experience, he may attract a mate who also has an inflexible will. When the first overflow of passionate love has been spent, the husband and wife may begin to look upon each other as competitors or rivals, rather than lovers or companions. In due time a situation will arise and create an impasse. If both members of the marriage refuse to yield, the result will be separation and bitterness — leaving a permanent scar upon the lives of each person, and casting a shadow upon the records of their souls. When both husband and wife are overly strong, their very strength may be the weakness in the marriage. However, if there is a basic or deep-rooted love, former life grace will enter the marriage; and the relentless pressures between two strong individuals, who refuse to admit defeat, will produce a superior degree of strength. Thereafter, such persons will respect one another, and revere the marriage relationship. In this, they will agree to direct and blend their similar, worthwhile attributes toward something fruitful, lasting, and good.

Formula: Time: Noon
Days: Ten

8. MANTRAM FOR MOTHER-TO-BE

Speak:—

> **I am a holy chalice or vessel of life—weaving, creating. The one standing near knows and weaves with me. I am strengthened; for I know the Plan never fails.**

Read: During the nine months of pregnancy, the former-life individuality of the one to be born overdwells the mother-to-be. In these months it is possible for both the mother-to-be and the child-to-be to absorb a certain knowledge of each other. Hence, the mother-to-be may take on some of the qualities of the individual to be born and, thus, during pregnancy she may undergo a noticeable change in temperament. All women have experienced the giving of birth in countless former lives. In some instances, women recover former-life memory of the mechanics of birth and, therefore, painless childbirth occurs. When the expectant mother and the individual to be born have trusted and loved one another in previous lives, the pre-birth experience and the giving of birth is a period of holy anticipation and joy.

Formula: Time: 3:30 p.m.
Days: Once a day during the entire period of pregnancy

9. Mantram to Welcome An Unborn Child

Speak:—
> **Beloved one: If it is the
> Will of the Father, let
> the flowing river of eternal
> life free you. Fear not
> the path of life. You are
> loved. You are welcomed
> with love.**

Read: When one prepares to re-embody on earth, he is sometimes repelled by his former-life debts awaiting expiation; the aggressive wills of those who would give him birth; or the strident and fearful conditions in the world. If one withdraws the desire to re-embody, the soul fails to furnish emanation and animation to the sacred atom within the heartbeat of the embryo. The result is a miscarriage or a stillborn child.

Formula: Time: Noon
     Days: One

10. Mantram for One Who Has Destroyed the Marriage Sheath

Speak:—

May the weight of darkness against my soul's light be translated through forgiving love. May I become a chaste, holy vessel for the channeling of pure love. If it is the Will of the Father, may I know reverence for all persons.

Read: In the earlier phases of marriage a husband and wife, through repeated sexual acts, build a marriage sheath. When either the husband or wife commits adultery, this sheath is permanently broken. And henceforth, something is ended which can never be restored. Thereafter, it will depend upon the choice of those in the marriage whether they shall remain together because of family opinions, children, mutual interests, or property. It is impossible for such persons to ever reclaim or inhabit the original sheath of their marriage. Persons are amoral because in many lives they have deviated from the ethic and morals protecting the purity of marriage. Those who disobey the Commandment, "Thou shalt not commit adultery," offend the Angels of Propagation, and violate the Law of God. No legal or physical law can cleanse an adulterous heart. All persons who commit adultery are scourged by their conscience, and must rectify their impure actions by hating their lusts, despising their sensuality, and grieving over their misspent passions. In time, they will turn to the just equation of God, and thus be cleansed and purified so that they may direct their passions as sacred instruments for reverent love.

Formula: Time: Noon
             Days: Ten

11. Mantramic Prayer To Be Said Before the Family Meal

Speak:—

Father, we thank Thee. We break this bread in remembrance of the Lord Jesus. May it nourish our bodies, so that we may better serve Thee.

Read: The mealtime can become a period of reverence and love. Unfortunately, the mealtime often sets the scene for family dissensions and quarrels. When one has a sensual appetite as to food, and a lack of reverence towards God, he expresses sentient gratification rather than gratitude during the mealtime. The mother and father who begin each meal with a blessing set a pattern of reverence and gratitude within the hearts and minds of their children.

Formula: Time: Before each meal

12. MANTRAM TO UNITE THE FAMILY

Speak:—

May there be peace in this home — peace of the Heavenly Helps. We call upon our Father. May He bless our home.

Read: Faith in God is a form of vitality. Parents who understand the miraculous vitality of faith in God instill this faith into their children; and the children are fortified for life. Spiritual nourishment in the home is a vital necessity to the parents and to each child. Parents may become more than parental authority to their children: loving parents may become symbols and interpreters of a loving Heavenly Father. The grace of former lives brings highly evolved persons together in families. The family which reflects the Holy Family is the family that believes in God, reveres Him, worships Him, and serves Him. Prayer in such a home is observed without shamefacedness or embarrassment. When pride stands between a family and the altar of prayer in the home, the home is a divided home.

Formula: Time: Sunset

PARENTS AND CHILDREN

13. MANTRAM TO GIVE CHILD SELF-ASSURANCE (AGE 7-9)

Child to speak:—

I will be more joyful each day. I am sure of my good.

Parent to Read: One way to discern that the etheric cord between the mother and child has been successfully detached is to observe the *wonder period* which begins in the child's 7th year. In this period, the child starts to rely upon his or her own innate power of perception, and thus begins an incessant questioning as to the "why" of things. If the parents will answer the child's questions with patience and truthfulness, the child will establish self-assurance and develop a retentive memory. The child's years of questioning are the preparation for a discerning mind in later life.

Formula: Time: On arising, and before sleep
               Days: Twenty-eight

14. Mantram To Teach Obedience
   (Age 7-9)

Child to speak:—
Each day I write a new song with my good.

Parent to Read: Those who have established authority in former lives enter the world respecting authority, and thus are obedient children in this life. When a child is disobedient and unruly, he endangers his own well-being, and disturbs the welfare of the home. Children not only need loving discipline, they thrive upon it. An orderly home is a disciplined household conducted by two parents who are concerned with the ultimate good for the family. When the rules of life are established with love during the dependent years, the child becomes a secure child and an obedient child. When a child intuits that his discipline is not authorized and agreed upon by both parents, he becomes confused and, therefore, less obedient. The child also intuits if the parents love one another; and responds to his parents' love as a secure and obedient child. To teach a child to observe the good in all people — and the good within all things — will free the faith and trust for the mature trials ahead.

Formula: Time: Before sleep
Days: Twenty-eight

15. Mantram for a Restless and Inattentive Child (Age 7-9)

Child to speak:

> **The trees, the sky, the wind, the water, all sing their songs. I am a good singer as I sing my song.**

Parent to Read: Due to former creative lives, some children are poets in their souls; and in this life they are delicate and sensitive. Such children often become restless and inattentive. Their studies suffer, and their parents are concerned. The lesser etheric body of a child is filled with incomprehensible vitality. Parents of restless and inattentive children should give their children some tangible means of channelling their restless vitality into creativity. Nature is a perfect nursemaid for sensitive and restless children. When these children are introduced to the creative wonders of nature's kingdom, they are free to release their imaginative processes and expressions.

Formula: Time: 3:30 p.m.
   Days: Twenty-eight

16. Mantram To Instill Responsiveness and Orderliness (Age 9-12)

Child to speak:—

> I am a happy, joyful one.
> I work each day until each
> task is done. My angel
> watches over me in night,
> in day.

Parent to read: Regardless of one's capabilities in a former life, he must relearn in each new embodiment the basic mechanics of two things: (1) how to take care of himself, and (2) how to get along with others. If one has established emotional harmony within himself in previous lives, he will begin in the 9th year to desire harmony in his relationships and environment. In this period the parents may utilize the momentum of the child's desire, and instill into the child a sense of responsibility, dignity, and co-operation. When a child has conscientiously consummated the tasks alloted to him in the home, the parents should give genuine praise to the child. Parents should be impartial in assigning and distributing the tasks within the home, so that each child may feel that he is doing his part. The home for the child is the miniature blueprint for his future relationships in the world. His sense of responsibility and his attitude toward those in the home will be later translated to his mature and adult world.

Formula: Time: 3:30 p.m.
Days: Twenty-eight

17. MANTRAM TO GIVE BIRTH TO THE APTITUDES AND TALENTS FROM FORMER LIVES (AGE 10-14)

Child to speak:

I am a creator in the world. Each day is new, and my part is joy.

Parent to read: Procrastination in a former life will incline a child during the puberty years to undergo a phase of unreality and detachment as to his studies and response to the disciplines within the home. During this period the parents should particularly devote themselves to sustain the child's interest in the part he is to play in the world. The transition period from childhood to individuality may become a time of self-discovery, and disclose some latent aptitudes or talents from previous lives.

Formula: Time: 3:30 p.m.
Days: Twenty-eight

18. Mantram to Overcome Self-Centeredness (Age 10-14)

Child to speak:—

I shall be considerate of others; and my lips shall speak with truth.

Parent to read: If in some previous life one has inherited command over many persons and possessions rather than earning command, and has failed to use the power of his wealth mercifully and charitably, he will enter the world in this life with a petulant and demanding attitude. He will expect to be the center of attention in this life; and he will feel the "world owes him something." Such overbearing persons in childhood are often the cause of anguish to thoughtful and conscientious parents; for the hapless parents are puzzled, knowing that these traits are not inherited from the ancestry or blood ties. In time, a child of this nature may benefit by the very grace of his association with considerate parents. However, if the parents are indulgent, the child will dominate the parents; and he will demand the center of the stage throughout life. Thus, he will become a "thorn in the flesh" of the family, and in all social relationships. Such a person accomplishes very little for himself in one life, and is the "cross" for others to bear.

Formula: Time: Before sleep
              Days: Twenty-eight

PARENTS AND CHILDREN

19. MANTRAM TO FREE CREATION IN A CHILD (Age 10-14)

Child to speak:—

My skills are better each day. I am trying. For I know there is a work for me in the world.

Parent to read:— When parents yearn and pray to give birth to a child, and look upon a child as a soul rather than the projection of their own traits, qualities, and aims, the Angels of Birth will entrust them with an exceptional child. Children born with special aptitudes have achieved a rhythmic accord with God's creation in their former lives. These children, who are eager to discover and to learn, are close to their souls' supervision. To wisely channel a child's former-life gifts requires much prayer and dedication on the part of the parent or parents. Parents should pray deeply for guidance, so that a wrong turn in the road be not made, or sacred time be lost.

Formula: Time: Before sleep
   Days: Twenty-eight

PARENTS AND CHILDREN

20. MANTRAM TO CORRECT A CHILD'S HABIT OF INTERRUPTING WHEN OTHERS ARE SPEAKING (Age 10-14)

Child to speak:—

I shall think of others when I speak. And my words shall be heard with love.

Formula: Time: 3:30 p.m.
Days: Thirty

21. MANTRAM TO RESPECT THE POSSESSIONS OF OTHERS (Age 14-16)

Youth to speak:—

Because everything I do affects someone else, I am thoughtful and kind. And I shall ask the angels to guide me and make me stronger each day.

Formula: Time: Before sleep
Days: Twenty-eight

22. MANTRAM TO TEACH A CHILD TO SHARE (Age 14-16)

Youth to speak:—

A loving one is an obedient one. A giving one is a receiving one. I am loving, and I play the game of life. And my angels help me to know God.

Formula: Time: 3:30 p.m.
Days: Twenty-eight

FEELINGS AND THOUGHTS

23. MANTRAM TO CLEANSE THE VESSEL OF LOVE, THE HEART

Speak:—

> **Father: Here is my heart,**
> **emptied of selfishness.**
> **May pure love enter in.**
> **And let me serve Thee.**

Read:— Throughout the ages the sacred atom within the heart has imprinted the feelings, thoughts, and actions of love. When the heart becomes a pure vessel for love, a perfect and flawless identity comes forth. Thoughts of fear, suspicion, and hate sully the expression of love — and love becomes distorted.

Formula: Time: Noon
   Days: Twenty-eight

24. Mantram to Fortify the Faith of This Life with the Faith of Former Lives

Speak:—

> **My faith as a pearl
> loses not its lustre.
> I am at home in God.
> My faith sustains me.**

Read:— Faith is an eternal attribute. Through faith one aligns himself with the Will of God. An unceasing faith is earned from fearless and proven actions in accord with the Will of God. He who has been obedient to the Laws of God in many former lives has perfect faith.

Formula: Time: On arising
Days: Ten

FEELINGS AND THOUGHTS

25. MANTRAM TO PURIFY THE EMOTIONS

Speak:—

**I look into the pure pool
of peace, and see the dove
flying above. It is my
soul's voice speaking of
God, and of the Real for me.**

Read:— The heart is a baptismal font of purification. When one dedicates for a better life, purification begins. And an inner and deeper quiet enters the heart. The voice of the soul may speak; and the thoughts begin to receive instruction from the higher worlds.

Formula: Time: Sunset
Days: Ten

26. Mantram to Renew Love Within the Heart

Speak:—

**The warming wonder of
healing grace beats
within my heart, and sets
my pace in joy, in love.**

Read:— Many former lives of selfishness and self-seeking produce a loveless heart. To quicken the heart's renewal of love, one should make the obvious gestures of love: consideration, tenderness, compassion. Thus the sacred atom within the heart will expand, and love will return. The heart is a spiritual, as well as a physical organ. It is the center of love's action. The denial of love's action, and the refusal to assume the responsibilities of love, will produce a loveless life — and the heart will become anguished, empty, void.

Formula: Time: Before sleep
Days: Twenty-eight

27. Mantram to Overcome Unrest and the Feeling of Homelessness

Speak:—

The storms of the senses are at rest. Light comes into each action. And strength comes forth to overcome the trials. I am at home in God.

Read:— Jesus said, *"The foxes have holes, and the birds of the air have nests; but the Son of man hath not where to lay his head."* (St. Matthew 8:20) Those who prepare for a higher stage of evolvement often find many of the accustomed landmarks removed and, for a time, become homeless ones. Such persons in the world are seeking their true brothers and sisters in the Christ. In time, they shall find their spiritual homeplace, and fulfill the words of Jesus, *"For whosoever shall do the will of my Father which is in heaven, the same is my brother, and sister, and mother."* (St. Matthew 12:50)

Formula: Time: Sunset
             Days: Ten

28. Mantram to Overcome Fear of Change

Speak:—

> **I welcome each new event with joy, and behold the living, loving life.**

Read:— The sound of one's prayers is as thunder in the World of God. When a person devotes himself to a more reverent life, he should be prepared for many changes to affect his habits, environment, and discrimination; for he is very close to experiencing certain areas of sensitivity in the heart and mind.

Formula: Time: 10 a.m.
Days: Twenty-eight

29. MANTRAM TO RECEIVE THE SOUL'S GRACE

Speak:—

My soul's medallion spreads its light. My thoughts are golden in the grace of pure thinking. Sustained by eternal love, I receive the True and the Real for me.

Read:— The medallion of the soul reflects the grace-record of good and virtuous actions from former lives. One receives this grace as pure thinking, and pure motive within feeling. Holy thoughts and pure emotions create a lucid field for thinking, so that one may receive the greater ideas, and channel loving works to the world. In meditation or in dreams, the soul may reflect to one the grace he has earned in former lives of sacrifice. When one lives a reverent and sacrificial life, he is the recipient of the grace of his soul.

Formula: Time: Before sleep
Days: Twenty-eight

30. Mantram to Overcome Contraclockwise Thinking

Speak:—

The clarity of my intent unfolds. The logic within truth presents the flawless perfection to me. I see things as they are. The Spirit of Truth instructs me now.

Read:— One inherits his intelligence from his ancestors, and his intellect from former lives. When a person has refused to face reality within his thoughts in former lives, or in this life, he sets up contraclockwise currents within the lesser etheric body. This creates a sequence of negative thoughts upon the area of the brain. Thus, the habit of negative thinking may become chronic, and cause extreme anguish, sorrow, and futility. When there is a tendency to be mystical in thinking, life is part dream and part necessity. When thoughts become inarticulate due to prejudice, the innermost feelings are warped and restrained.

Formula: Time: Before sleep
             Days: Twenty-eight

31. Mantram to Overcome Emotional Tensions

Speak:—

> **I release all tensions
> and let the storm within
> come to rest in the clear
> pool of my soul's quiet.
> Peace.**

Read:— Excessive pride in former lives develops an egotistical shell, and one enters the world with many dormant emotional tensions. These are expressed as self-centeredness and self-satisfied complacencies, preventing direct experience with what the present life has to offer. The egotistical shell stands between a person and the soul's action. Thus, undefined tensions occur in temperament, personality, and body. Sometimes much suffering is required to dissolve the egotistical shell.

Formula: Time: Sunset
             Days: Fifteen

32. Mantram to Overcome Mental Tensions

Speak:—

> **I accept my timing as of
> the Will of God. I order
> the pattern of my days to
> the Plan of God. In this,
> I know peace; I know love.**

Read:— Mental tensions are the result of a strong will seeking a creative channel. Mental tensions are expressed as impatience, quickness to anger, impulsive actions, irrational or snap judgments. One may begin creative action with the soul's faculties when he releases all feelings of possessivism, and overcomes prejudging thoughts.

Formula: Time: 10. a.m.
Days: Fifteen

33. Mantram to Overcome Fear of Slander

Speak:—

I cease listening to the clamors. Truth, clear and sweet, speaks to me. With courage, I see the Real, and live in harmony to that which my soul seeks.

Read:— Negative inferences move telepathically into familiar grooves of one's conscience. These grooves of conscience, built from wrongdoing in this life and former lives, make one receptive to the negative thoughts of others. While one may seem to be maligned, misunderstood, or falsely accused, he should seek inwardly to learn what is speaking through vilification, slander, or gossip. Pure motive and true intent will open the resources of the soul's grace; and thus insulate one from slander, and bring vision and renewed peace. *"Blessed are ye, when men shall revile you, and persecute you, and shall say all manner of evil against you falsely, for my sake."* (St. Matthew 5:11)

Formula: Time: Morning on arising, and at sunset
Days: Thirty

34. Mantram to Overcome Manipulation

Speak:—
> **I blend with the need, and
> work with the tides of men.
> In peace I stand. And in
> strength I serve. Let Light
> light my way.**

Read:— In the world there are, unfortunately, many who believe in the power of force, pressure, or manipulation. The individual who is inclined to expect a windfall, or to receive without earning, becomes a victim to such persons, and may start an avalanche of negative actions, thereby delaying grace. To remain serene and untroubled, one should learn the culture of contentment, acceptance, and more — of absorbing industry. Thus he will live within a state of continuing creativity, which provides protection against cupidity and acquisition. All lasting and indestructible things are purchased by sacrifice, industry, and faith in God.

Formula: Time: Sunset
Days: Thirty

35. Mantram to See Clearly the Issue at Hand

Speak:—

My soul speaks to me of the greater ultimate. I shall not fear, but I shall also be not deceived! For truth shall release me into the Good for all near and by me.

Read:— The soul seeks, in many and different ways, to reveal the immortal and eternal purpose of man. Each age speaks in a different manner to man. God has so willed it that one believes each life to be the most vital. When it is understood that life is everlasting, and that one must in each life incorporate the concepts of the age, period, and time, while yet remaining essentially the same, he learns to become observer as well as actor in the drama of life. When all persons in the world fully understand reincarnation and re-embodiment, they will then learn to hate less, censure less, and to love more. To overcome hidden fears of the unknown, and to receive an inner poise as related to the seeming injustices in the world, one should believe in God's law of perfect justice and balance, and know that the formula for life will be revealed in time through the soul's action.

Formula: Time: Sunset
              Days: Ten

36. Mantram to Prevent Dejection in Thought

Speak:—

**The wounds of yesterday are
healed within the joy of
today. My wounds give me
remembrance of the wounds
of the Lord Jesus. So that
I may heal others, may I
stand in His Love and Light.**

Read:— An embittered mind develops a reaction within the lesser etheric body. An excessive moisture similar to unshed tears begins to form, creating a chronic spasm of dejection which occurs at repeated intervals. When one prolongs thoughts of bitterness, and retains fixed ideas as to seeming injustices in the world, he creates an environment unpleasant to himself, and uninviting to others. Each time a person blames another for some painful circumstance in his life, he opens an old groove in the lesser etheric body, and thus etches more deeply his feeling of injustice and bitterness. One should determine to erase forever the belief that any event in his life was caused by any one person; for God's justice cannot fulfill its action when one thinks continually with a judging mind. The highest degree of life's expression is the human will. By turning the will to the Will of God, one may change embittered thought currents into healing grace and love.

Formula: Time: Sunset
              Days: Ten

37. MANTRAM TO OVERCOME FEAR

Speak:—

There is Light around me and of me. I shall fear not. My heart shall be steady with fearlessness, for I know the Father holds the key to the plan for me.

Read:— A mind filled with fear is an indecisive mind. Timidity is the beginning of fear. When one learns to trust the Rhythm of God, he will discern the higher order and plan of life. A person who is continually and repeatedly fearful devitalizes certain delicate sheaths in the lesser etheric body. To mend these etheric sheaths, one should strive to increase the light in his thoughts, and thus align himself with the pure, sweet rhythm of the soul. The soul responds in perfect timing, and helps one to behold the plan unique in his evolvement. True earnestness, devotion, and repeated prayer will produce a continued oneness with the living, eternal life.

Formula: Time: Sunset
Days: Twenty-eight

38. Mantram to Overcome Fear

Speak:—

All things are ordered in my pattern, and I fear not. For I know there is no power greater than love.

Read:— Man is embodied in the Eternal God. When one knows he is eternal, he is released from fear of the unknown. *"Fear not, litle flock; for it is your Father's good pleasure to give you the kingdom."* (St. Luke 12:32) No one is exempt from fear. All minor fears stem from one basic fear: isolation from God, and failure to remember the Will of God. Fear of moving objects, of persons, of lack, of competition, of loss of health, all are resolved when one knows God Is. Those who fearlessly pray for peace should continue and continue in prayer, for the prayers of many dedicated persons make less harsh the darkened wills of men. And though the axis of the earth may tremble, He Who is the Mighty God shall not be moved.

Formula: Time: Sunset
             Days: Twenty-eight

39. Mantram to Channel Purity

Speak:—

**Into my thoughts come the
mirrored patterns of the Real.
I claim only the jewels pure,
and set them free in the
diadem of my soul's light.**

Read:— Purity is an accomplishment of the ages. A person with a childlike heart and mind is rarely at home in a materialistic world. The soul of a pure person often prompts him to embody into a calloused environment with thoughtless and selfish people. Until the essential meaning of the present life is disclosed to him, he will suffer from bewilderment and desperate loneliness. God plants the pure person as a seed in coarse environments so that men may believe in good.

Formula: Time: Sunset
Days: Twenty-eight

40. Mantram to Recover the Eternal Patience

Speak:—

**I am a creator in God.
I call my answer to me
out of my need.**

Read:— In God's divine economy, there is no superfluous action; in each life man experiences only that which he needs and can utilize. No one in the physical world is as yet perfect. Each person has countless lives and innumerable ages before him in which to achieve perfection. When this is understood, one may work with *eternal patience*.

Formula: Time: Sunset
             Days: **Ten**

41. Mantram to Clarify Confused Concepts

Speak:—

Where I search, my soul shall reach; and the answer long sought will come. I shall know and stand with God.

Read:— A person who seeks with a reverent and knowing heart enlarges the capacity of the soul's action. And the miracle of the Undiscovered Self will be revealed.

Formula: Time: Sunset
Days: Fifteen

42. MANTRAM TO ILLUMINE THE THOUGHTS

Speak:—

In the innermost part of my heart the eternal flame burns, and the Light moves. And in the stillness of my thoughts Light spreads.

Formula: Time: Sunset
Days: Twenty-eight

43. MANTRAM TO ACCEPT THE PATTERN OF LIFE

Speak:—

My will is fulfilled in love-giving. I will create the mosaic of preciousness. And I shall strike the note of harmony in each way of doing!

Formula: Time: Sunset
Days: Twenty-eight

44. Mantram to Overcome Distrust

Speak:—

> **The walls of separateness—built from the little fears of men—now open to my serving and my giving. I blend my love's effort with peace.**

Formula: Time: Sunset
Days: Thirty

45. Mantram to Overcome Scattered Thinking

Speak:—

The Way has begun, and the zigzag trial is done. The work in Light and the skills in love blend themselves in heart and mind. The joyous dance of life begins in rhythmic harmony. The peace is spoken. The Light comes forth. And the joyous note arises.

Formula: Time: 10 a.m.
Days: Twenty

46. Mantram to Overcome Dwelling Upon the Past

Speak:—

My golden hope is renewed each day, for I have tried. I shall go forth with the forward look. And I shall be armored with love.

Formula: Time: 3:30 p.m.
               Days: Twenty-eight

WORK AND SERVING

47. MANTRAM TO ACCEPT VOCATIONAL RESPONSIBILITIES

I work in my grace, and weary not. For I know no burden is greater than my grace.

Formula: Time: Noon
            Days: Ten

48. MANTRAM TO WORK JOYFULLY

Whatever the day speaks to me, my soul knows the answer. I set my pace to the timing of God. I am eager and alert to do the Father's Will.

Formula: Time: On arising
            Days: Ten

DRAUGHTS OF REMEMBRANCE

49. MANTRAM FOR ADVANCEMENT IN WORK

Thank God for growth. In my serving I give of myself, and rejoice as I increase the good.

Formula: Time: Noon
Days: Ten

50. MANTRAM TO ACCEPT CHANGE

I shall stand strong in circumstance, and peaceful in destiny. Grace is my freedom.

Formula: Time: Noon
Days: Ten

51. Mantram to Become A Joyous Presence in the Working Environment

I sing praises with a new voice, a new vowel — speaking the tongue of the new age.

Formula: Time: On arising
           Days: Twenty-eight

52. Mantram to Develop A Vital Interest in One's Occupation

The Eternal Knowing within me accepts the terms of my liberty. In seeking and fulfilling the Right and the Light, I shall be instructed by the soul day by day.

Formula: Time: On arising
           Days: Ten

53. Mantram to Overcome Resistance to Work

The mist is removed. The Light reveals my way. I stand and send my call to serve in Light and Love.

Formula: Time: Noon
             Days: Ten

54. Mantram to Clarify Serving

My dedication to serve awakens the will to know. I hear from the deep within, the guidance for the way to serve in the Light.

Formula: Time: Noon
             Days: Ten

55. MANTRAM TO OVERCOME CONFUSION IN WORKING ENVIRONMENT

My harmony speaks to me above the clamors and the din. I hear the Music of the Spheres, and know it to be the voice of my soul.

Formula: Time: Noon
Days: Ten

56. MANTRAM FOR A DEDICATED WORKER

If it is the Will of the Father, may I serve and work to bring order into this environment. And may I make alignment to the purpose of this labor. May the Angels of Industry, working with the Father, bring order, peace, purpose, to each one.

Formula: Time: Noon
Days: Ten

152   DRAUGHTS OF REMEMBRANCE

57. MANTRAM TO OVERCOME DISSENSION IN WORK ENVIRONMENT

May the fiery wounds of wrong wordings be anointed and healed in Light. And may the miracles of my soul manifest joyful speaking.

Formula: Time: Noon
            Days: Ten

58. MANTRAM TO ESTABLISH A NEW RHYTHM IN EXPECTANCY

The wondrous reality in God reveals itself to me. I work willingly. I serve joyously, awaiting the Plan in God to come forth.

Formula: Time: Noon
            Days: Ten

59. Mantram to Overcome Fear of Loss of Employment

I have command of my necessity. Each day I am sustained in my Eternal Good.

Formula: Time: Noon
　　　　　　Days: Ten

60. Mantram to Prosper

I have sown the seed. And the measure of the harvest fulfills the intent and Will of God.

Formula: Time: On arising
　　　　　　Days: Twenty-eight

61. Mantram for Wise Stewardship

God's plan of economy works for me. The treasures of my soul's good come forth to enrich and prosper me on the way.

Formula: Time: On arising
Days: Twenty-eight

62. Mantram to Overcome Tensions in Employment

My skills are unwavering. Perfect justice reveals the way for all. As the pattern unfolds, I am joyful.

Formula: Time: Noon
Days: Ten

63. Mantram to Receive Promotion in Right Timing

I serve lovingly. I spread my orbit each day and hasten not. Events shape their course for me, for my soul alone knows my true promise, my timing.

Formula: Time: Noon
Days: Ten

64. Mantram to Rise Above Humdrum or Monotonous Tasks in Work

Each day is a genius, and each day a marvel. I work. I seek. I stand. How vast my kingdom is in Love, in Light.

Formula: Time: Sunset
Days: Ten

65. MANTRAM TO OPEN DOORS TO NEW EMPLOYMENT

Each day I build the perfect peace, that I may find the perfect place, and way, to love, to serve.

Formula: Time: On arising
Days: Twenty-eight

66. MANTRAM TO HARMONIZE THE EMOTIONS IN CONFINING WORK

I trust and work and love and serve.

Formula: Time: Noon
Days: Ten

67. Mantram to Release Creative Gifts and Works

Beauty comes forth and is fulfilled in every part of me. I am strong and I dedicate to serve God.

Formula: Time: Noon
Days: Ten

68. Mantram to Translate Talent into Creation

My reed now sends its note. I make a joyful sound. Creation. Creativity. Create!

Formula: Time: Noon
Days: Ten

69. MANTRAM TO RESPOND TO THE INVISIBLE HELPS OF THE SOUL

The angels go before me, preparing my way. The tensions are dissolved. And the Greater Plan is triumphant.

Formula: Time: On arising
Days: Twenty-eight

HEALING

70. MANTRAM OF DEDICATION TO HEAL OTHERS

Love enfolds me. Wisdom enlightens me. May my hands be blessed in their healing works. Christ is my vision, my wisdom.

Formula: Time: Sunset
Days: Twenty-eight

71. MANTRAM TO HEAL DEPLETION

I channel God's Mighty Power in renewed strength. I fortify my labors and increase my capacities.

Formula: Time: Noon
Days: Five

72. Mantram to Heal the Wounds of the Past

I am strong in the Light. My soul is the open door to the Real. Each day something of love is fulfilled.

Formula: Time: Sunset
Days: Ten

73. Mantram for Acceptance of the Lesson in Chronic Ailment

The grace of my good illumines my thought. I fear not. I am grateful for this experience.

Formula: Time: On arising, and at sunset
Days: Ten

HEALING

74. MANTRAM TO REVEAL THE CAUSE OF SICKNESS

I believe in the Will of the Father for me. I gather my grace within the lesson of this experience, and fear not.

Formula: Time: On arising
Days: Ten

75. MANTRAM TO BUILD VITALITY

The blessed Way guides me as I cheerfully fulfill each task of the day. The organs of my body respond to the Healing Will of God.

Formula: Time: Sunset
Days: Twenty-eight

76. MANTRAM TO HEAL TENSION

> **I am centered in peace — healing peace. In Christ, tension cannot be.**

Formula: Time: On arising
            Days: Twenty-eight

77. MANTRAM TO CO-ORDINATE THE MUSCLES OF THE BODY

> **My will surrenders to the Greater Will. I blend with the true meaning of the now, and sing with joy; for hope cometh on the morn.**

Formula: Time: On arising
            Days: Twenty-eight

78. MANTRAM TO CLARIFY THE VISION

My vision is of the soul. I see with the eyes of the Sacred Self. I am patient, awaiting the unfolding of God's Plan.

Formula: Time: Sunset
Days: Twenty-eight

79. MANTRAM TO DISCLOSE THE CAUSE OF CONTINUED ALLERGIES

My soul removes the barriers built by the little will's wrong desirings. I free my life and my will to the need. I am loving, joyous, free.

Formula: Time: Noon
Days: Twenty-eight

80. MANTRAM TO HEAL STRAINED RELATIONSHIPS

Let my words be healing words. And let my actions manifest the healing Light.

Formula: Time: Sunset
Days: Twenty-eight

81. MANTRAM TO OVERCOME THE TENDENCY TO BE DOMINANT

I await the Lord's Way for me. The indwelling Light stills my little will. I stand strong, yet gentle and tender. I heal.

Formula: Time: On arising
Days: Twenty-eight

82. MANTRAM TO RELEASE THE HEALING POWER OF THE SOUL

**How gentle my peace.
How loving my tenderness.
In healing grace, I set
my countenance, my face,
toward Light.**

Formula: Time: Sunset
           Days: Twenty-eight

SLEEP AND THE SOUL

83. MANTRAM TO RECEIVE GUIDANCE FOR THE DAY

**My soul has mastered the
veil of night and sleep.
With guidance on the morn,
I arise to my labors in
Light, and fear not the
action of the day.**

Formula: Time: On arising
            Days: Twenty-eight

84. MANTRAM TO STRENGTHEN THE WIL ON THE MORN

**I arise on this new day
renewed and new again.
The tensions among the
skills of men shall defeat
me not.**

Formula: Time: On arising
            Days: Ten

85. MANTRAM FOR ACCEPTANCE OF THE DAY'S PLAN

> I claim the golden guidance
> on the morn from the remembrance of the night. I
> blend my works of sleep with
> the waking day. Joyously,
> I recall the Eternal's Plan
> for me in this eternity.

Formula: Time: On arising
Days: Twenty-eight

86. MANTRAM TO EXTERNALIZE UNKNOWN AND HIDDEN CAPACITIES

> In effortless effort I
> stand, loving the way
> of the morning's light;
> for the memory of the
> night's action in sleep
> strengthens me and sends
> me on.

Formula: Time: On arising
Days: Ten

87. Mantram to Overcome Dread of the Day

I arise joyously to the day, and accept each thing as of the Plan for me.

Formula: Time: On arising
Days: Ten

88. Mantram to Harvest the Soul's Grace After the Night's Sleep

The grace of the day awaits my channelling.

Formula: Time: On arising
Days: Ten

89. MANTRAM TO SUSTAIN THE HEALING STRENGTH GAINED IN THE NIGHT'S SLEEP

I make my walk in the song of my soul's Light.

Formula: Time: On arising
Days: Ten

90. MANTRAM TO RECEIVE THE SOUL'S INSTRUCTION

May I be led to where I may best serve in the night. May my labors of the night become the daytime works of Light.

Formula: Time: Before sleep
Days: Twenty-eight

91. MANTRAM TO RISE ABOVE THE LOWER DREAM VEILS

If it is the Will of the Father, may I open my heart to the soul's work during sleep. May my body of the earth, faithful in its work, be surrounded by protective peace. May my soul's Light and love direct me to receive instruction in the night.

Formula: Time: Before sleep
Days: Twenty-eight

SLEEP AND THE SOUL

92. MANTRAM FOR PURE DREAM SYMBOLS

**I go into the place my soul
has prepared for me. I
fear not. And I will bring
forth, on the morn, memory of
the night's work and help.
If it is the Will of the
Father, let direct guidance
come unto me.**

Formula: Time: Before sleep
              Days: Twenty-eight

93. MANTRAM TO OVERCOME SLEEPLESSNESS AND FEAR OF THE NIGHT

**I see God in all things.
Regardless of the night,
I believe in the Light
and the Will of God.**

Formula: Time: Before sleep
              Days: Twenty-eight

94. Mantram to Bring Coherence to Dreams

I serve and love, and seal in the Real. For my soul's grace now opens the day and the night.

Formula: Time: Before sleep
             Days: Ten

95. Mantram to Ascertain the Soul's Reality As Experienced in Sleep

Tonight I will seek to labor in the Light, and thus renew my plan of action for the morn. Light heals, frees, and sustains me. Peace. Peace. Peace.

Formula: Time: Before sleep
             Days: Ten

SLEEP AND THE SOUL

96. Mantram to Overcome Fear of the Unknown Portals of Sleep

May the Angel of Sleep awaken me on the morn. May I awaken joyous and refreshed. I fear neither life nor death. I am.

Formula: Time: Before sleep
Days: Twenty-eight

97. Mantram for Protection During Sleep

In the night and the day I am in the Presence of the Light. My Father's protections surround me. I call on my good Guardian to bless my life and all my works.

Formula: Time: Before sleep
Days: Ten

98. MANTRAM TO COME CLOSER TO THE ETERNAL ASPECTS OF THE SOUL

I hold the Eternal Thread and release it not. I command the entanglements of my lesser will. Let the Light in me remain immortal, free!

Formula: Time: Before sleep
Days: Ten

99. MANTRAM TO RESPOND TO THE SOUL'S GUIDANCE

My rest, my peace, are as the quiet blue sea. My soul times my action. I will obey the Eternal Plan, and serve.

Formula: Time: Before sleep
Days: Ten

100. MANTRAM FOR HEALING DURING SLEEP

**My love is my leading.
My soul sends me into
the Path of the Pure,
fulfilling my lesson
and way for now.**

Formula: Time: Before sleep
Days: Ten

SUMMARY

GOD'S MIGHTY JUSTICE AND PERFECT MERCY

The draughts of remembrance, the dream symbols of past lives, and the intermittent reminders of former lives are a natural part of the little-known processes within man's consciousness. Prayer and meditation unite man with God. Mantramic speaking unites him with his soul and the records of his soul. A reverent attitude toward his mission and purpose in life enables man to give birth to the noble impulses of past lives.

The majority of persons expiate their debts from former lives, and receive their lessons from past lives through painful events, crises, tragedies, sacrifices, and sorrows. Each crisis in life is a nudge from the soul. God's mighty justice, working with the soul, times the crises

SUMMARY

in one's life. God's perfect mercy enables one to withstand the crises and the trials. Through His perfect mercy, each trial is accompanied by a miraculous blessing or compensation and, in some instances, one may receive a revelation or illumination.

A person who sees life as eternal has overcome the fear of life and death, and he moves rhythmically with the soul's timing and the mighty laws of God. When one willingly exerts the effort to comply with the greater laws of God, rather than conform to the lesser wills of men, he will triumph over the major crises and calamities of the world; the tragedies, disappointments, and sorrows in human events; and the defeats and frustrations in the personal life. With the help of the Recording Angels, his soul will open to him the Book of Eternal Life, wherein is revealed the knowledge of past lives and of lives to come.

THE END